AIR, SUNLIGHT AND A BIT OF LAND

AIR, SUNLIGHT AND A BIT OF LAND

by

MARIAN LOWE QUACKENBUSH

YE GALLEON PRESS
FAIRFIELD, WASHINGTON

Library of Congress Cataloging in Publication Data

Quackenbush, Marian Lowe, 1901-
Air, sunlight, and a bit of land.

Includes index.
1. Quackenbush, Marian Lowe, 1901- . 2. Quackenbush family. 3. Owyhee River Valley—Social life and customs. 4. Owyhee River Valley—Biography. I. Title.
F882.098Q3 1982 979.5'97041'0924[B] 82-13441
ISBN 0-87770-275-6

TABLE OF CONTENTS

Marian Lowe, Age Three, 1904

Marian Lowe-Sophomore, Whitman College

INTRODUCTION

Marian (Lowe) Quackenbush is a native of Eastern Oregon and has spent most of her life in that area or in Eastern Washington.

She lived on three different homesteads and on at least that many different irrigated farms where the Owyhee River was the source, or anticipated source, of irrigation. She saw that source augmented by a small man-made dam and later by the huge Owyhee Dam in the canyon of the river. This dam was a fore-runner of the Grand Coulee Dam on the Columbia in Washington.

After her elementary and high school years were over, she entered Whitman College in Walla Walla, Washington, graduating in 1923 with a B.A. degree, Magna Cum Laude and Phi Beta Kappa. A few years of teaching followed graduation and her marriage to Carl Quackenbush. The young couple then moved to and settled in Spokane, Washington where they have lived since 1926.

She maintained her legal ties and her personal interests in the Mitchell Butte Hot Springs farm held for so many years by her family until the distance between it and Spokane caused her to sell it in 1975.

Many of her mother's interests show in her adult activities, particularly in those connected with educational backgrounds. She has always enjoyed and helped with the work of the Parent Teacher Association. She was president of the Longfellow grade school and North Central high school P.T.A.'s. She was a long-time member and president of the Spokane Branch of the American Association of University Women. She is a member of P.E.O., which organization has long been known for its support of Cottey College in Nevada, Missouri. She is a member of St. Andrew's Episcopal Church in Spokane, and is one of the lay readers there.

While her children were in school, she was quite active giving book reviews for many church, social and philanthropic organizations, often having two or more engagements in a single day.

Marian and Carl Quackenbush 50th Wedding Anniversary

Marian Lowe Quackenbush Surrounded by Her Family, 1982

ACKNOWLEDGEMENTS

Life on the Owyhee was never dull, but the stories of those years would not have been told as they happened in the Lowe household had it not been for the encouragement received from two women whose zeal and whose technical skills neither faded nor faltered. Over a period of approximately three years, Mildred Elliot, a former teacher at the Owyhee School has written letter after letter, has looked for sources, and always, again and again, through sickness and death in her own family, and in mine, encouraged and sympathized with me.

The other friend whose work and "words of Wisdom" have been invaluable, as is her clerical skill, is Doris Brown of Spokane, and of St. Andrew's Church. At just the right time for getting me "on the job again," Doris would share of her strength with me. Largely due to her "you can do it" attitude, my children, grandchildren and great-grandchildren will learn how life was lived in those long ago days on "raw" but promising land. It wasn't always easy, but there was love and compassion. What could be better?

CHAPTER 1

The Homestead Act, the first of a series of acts and amendments which make up the national homestead law, was passed by Congress in 1862 after the first free homestead bill was drafted and introduced in 1846. This act provided that a tract not exceeding 160 acres of unappropriated portions of the public domain should be given to any head of a family who would live on the tract for five years and improve it. The provisions of the law extended also to any person 21 years of age who is a citizen of the United States or has filed declaration of his intention to become a citizen.

Within ten years, 28 million acres were "homesteaded" under this act, and the procedure continued on into the 20th Century. In fact, Horace Greeley (1811-72) of the *New York Tribune* who was hospitable to all of the new movements reaching toward a new world in which men and women might lead free and happy lives, gave the famous advice, "Go West, young man, go West." With George Henry Evans he insisted that every man had the same natural right to a bit of land, as to air and sunlight. Evans and Greeley fought for a free homestead from the public domain to every settler, for limitation of the size of individual holdings, and for no alienation of the homestead (no legal attachment that would prevent the homesteader from keeping his land), voluntary or otherwise.

Individual states passed laws to control the situations as they arose. Many western states exempted a man's homestead from confiscation to pay the owner's debts...in other words, his house, no matter how humble, was his castle.

Amounts of allowable land varied in different states. The "improving" of the homestead was subject to varying interpretations: how large must a house be, and of what materials (were tar-paper shacks acceptable?), must there be a well? What provisions must be made for stoves and fuels in order for the family to maintain a home in winter? Could a cow or horse exist? How about chickens? What crops were acceptable, and how many acres were required to be in crops?

In areas where there was insufficient rainfall to produce crops of quality and quantity for sale or use in maintaining livestock or people, it was necessary to find or improvise access to water in sufficient supply to satisfy the legal requirements for "proving up" before the land could be deeded to the homesteaders. Was the homesteader claiming to qualify under 3-year law, 27-month law, or how? The less time that he allowed himself, the more improvements and payments he must make. Fortunately (or unfortunately, as the case might be) the homesteader himself did not have to remain on the land if he could find a paying job somewhere else and *if* his wife and/or children would live there in his absence and claim the homestead as their home. It staggers the mind to imagine the problems that must have arisen from such arrangements. What about sickness? scarcity of food? or lack or loss of a horse and some sort of conveyance? What about schooling for the children? It added up to a high price, other than in terms of dollars.

The reasons why people came west varied with the geographical growth and the population of the United States. They were threaded through with the idealism of missionaries, the struggles leading up to and through the Civil War, the desire for the wealth that seemed to be easily available and the hope of a new kind of life for thousands of immigrants, thrifty and hardy, who came in groups from the far eastern states after having left their original homelands. In the eastern part of the country the professions were already being threatened with being in over-supply. Why not go west, why not get land, why not establish oneself and one's family where there was room for growth? Thus, doctors, ministers, bankers, lawyers, store-keepers, teachers, surveyors, musicians, already some government workers, as well as specialized farmers including dairymen and cattlemen, and artisans in many fields came west, settled in eastern and central Oregon and Idaho and proceeded to establish homes. Not all land could be utilized as homestead cropland. Thousands of acres were dryland acreage, used by the cattle and sheep barons. These tremendous "spreads" were not the "bit of land" envisioned the Homestead Act and laws.

The ingenious homesteaders—visionary, hardworking, occasionally well-trained, but oftentimes in possession of only minimal skills—sometimes worked with family members or neighbors to prepare a small reservoir from an available spring or, after a few years, from a well in order to have enough water to sustain not only human life but also a few head of stock and flocks. In other cases, as in Malheur County, some amazingly well-executed, comprehensive and ingenious irrigation systems were built. Access to water, especially from the Malheur and Owyhee rivers and Willow and Bully creeks, made water distribution possible, which changed homesteads to attractive, productive farms. The scalloped banks of irrigation ditches added their characteristic lines to the topography while miles of Lombardy poplars outlined individual acreages, corrals, or stock yards. Plots of fast-growing, tough and thorny locusts provided posts for fencing. From the very first arrival the homesteaders looked ahead toward self-sufficiency. The more commonly descriptive word for "air, sunlight and a bit of land" was a 'diversified' farm, which was made possible by the addition of water to that "bit of land." The task of providing water—even for household use—ran the gamut from, at the first, carrying a tight-woven canvas bag of water from a hook or nail on a wagon-box (where the travel motion might provide a cooling effect on the water) or, from a stout nail or spike from a tree limb or fence post, or corner on a tent or house—any location chosen to help the air movement and evaporation cool the water to make it more palatable instead of merely wet. More and more ingenious and efficient methods were used, culminating at last in running water for the house and irrigation for the fields. It required the foresight of a dreamer, the faith that the dream could be fulfilled, and the hard work, perseverance and determination of family groups to endure hardships they encountered for a considerable number of years until they could reach the point where mere existence could develop into a worthwhile and satisfying way of life, albeit one that offered few conveniences.

Possibly the most joyful experiences afforded the homesteaders came from finding some other person or family in the area who had the same background (geographical, racial, occupational, educational or religious.) It wasn't necessary to "take a liking" to the new persons—although that helped—but as C.S. Lewis has said, "People who know a lot of the same things can hardly help talking about them," and of course talking about one's similarities helps to bring understanding which, in turn, smooths many a rough path. It used to be said that the farther away one's nearest neighbor lived, the more sure one should be to learn the way to that home immediately. In case of illness, shortage of food or any other need, the shortest and easiest way from one home to the other should be known.

When the inevitable question came, "Where are you from?" and my father said, "I'm from Kansas," the way was opened for a whole series of stories, adventures and history—incidentally giving my father an opportunity to tell the first, but far from the last, repetition of the story of his birth. It was his favorite story, although it was somewhat embarrassing to my mother, who always seemed to feel that it contained a touch of blasphemy! (Father always said, "Jesus Christ was born in a stable, but I was born in a granary!") Like most family histories, it started "a way back when" in Scotland, where the family name was "Loch," or some similar derivation of "lake"—not becoming "Lowe" until the family arrived near St. Louis, Missouri. "Sandy" Lowe was an orphan. He married Elizabeth Stowe of western Missouri. He soon became embroiled in the struggles between the North and South in the Civil War, hoping to add his strength, courage and leadership to help make Kansas "free." Like a good many other leaders, he received the nickname "Cap" and was known as one of the Northerners who with his men were marked for extermination. By moving from location to location, he kept out of the clutches of the nearby southerners. "Cap Sandy" Lowe developed a farm near Lawrence, Kansas, where he built a rather large home and proceeded to produce an also rather large family. It is reported that his first child, named Tom, died very young. Henry was the second child. Next came two girls. After that came triplet girls, Louella, Louisa, and Letitia. At this time Elizabeth Lowe, with her brood of little ones headed by the oldest boy, was attempting to manage the farm, and the children, while preparing for another birth. "Sandy" returned to his farm, his house and family whenever a break in the fighting permitted.

At the outbreak of the Civil War, an American guerilla commander who had lived as a gambler by the name of Charley Hart, taught school for one year while in Kansas, then embarked on a criminal career including horse-stealing and murder. He now led a troop of Confederate irregulars and received a captain's commission under the name "Quantrell" (pronounded Quan-trill.) He and "Cap Sandy" were sworn enemies. He knew where "Cap" Lowe's farm and home were located about ten miles south of Lawrence and vowed to destroy it. At dawn on August 21, 1863, Quantrell, with 450 men raided Lawrence, pillaged the town and slaughtered over 150 men, women and children—arriving at "Cap Sandy" Lowe's farm in the evening. The oldest Lowe boy was in bed with typhoid fever. Quantrell gave an order for the men to start a fire to burn the house. Some of his followers rounded up the children and with their mother, took them to the farm granary. Quantrell said they had no reason to waste time and effort in getting the sick boy out of the house. His attitude was that he and his men had killed many people already that day, so why hesitate at one more?

Dissension arose among his troops. Some of his men said they had not come on this expedition to kill defenseless sick boys, and pregnant women whose time for delivery had come. The more decent among his men threatened to break away from the main group saying they would carry the sick boy and would help his mother and the children into the granary. Over Quantrell's protests, this plan was carried out, and sometime in the middle of the night or in the early morning of the 22nd of August a baby boy was born.

"Sandy," who had never quite recovered from the loss of his first born child, Thomas, insisted that this new baby should also be named "Thomas" with the addition of a second name, "Marion," for a man about whom Sandy had studied and for whom he had great admiration. This Marion had fought in the Indian wars. He had been a delegate to the provincial congress of 1775. He became a Lieutenant Colonel in the Continental Army. His troops made up the only important American forces in South Carolina, his native state. He was called the "Swamp Fox." He filled an unexpired term in the state senate, then retired from public life in 1790. It is easy to understand how a man like Marion would capture the fancy of a young Scotsman in Kansas. Both fought for their country, although in different eras, and Sandy had the very opposite type of example before him in the renegade Quantrell. What a contrast! So "Thomas Marion" was my father's name! Henry, the oldest, survived the typhoid fever and when the mother died later on, he and the other children—especially the older girls—helped to raise the younger members of the family.

It was a stroke of fortune that Sandy met and married a young widow, Julia Jamieson, who had a crippled son who needed medical attention. The two families were soon joined and in due time a girl, Blanche, was born to Sandy and Julia. Julia originally came from northwest Missouri, a member of the Forbes community near Butler. This numerous clan boasted members with every type of background, but, in addition to farmers and small businessmen and pharmacists, they claimed an unusually large number of men in the professions: doctors and lawyers especially, plus teachers and ministers. The homes of these men displayed books galore, and usually musical instruments of various kinds.

By the age of 14, Sandy had read and absorbed a book of etiquette, and in his maturity had definite ideas about the training of his children. His boys were all to choose a vocation—a way to earn a living in addition to working a farm—a vocation that could be used in almost any situation. The young Thomas Marion ("Tom" or "T.M.") chose carpentry and must

The Young Flora Belle Forbes (about age 22)

have had very good training, for he was an excellent carpenter. Evidence of his skill showed in the results he turned out, wherever he lived. He had little formal education but was fortunate to have been in school at a time when the teacher was supposed to teach the children everything that he, himself, knew in his specialties, instead of following rigid grade lines. For instance, one of Tom's teachers, a man, was much interested in mathematics, so Tom had training in elementary math, plus algebra, and "higher" mathematics. He also acquired considerable knowledge of surveying and in his mature years had some fine instruments that came into good use in "locating" land boundaries.

Julia, his stepmother, needed help in getting her crippled son to the attention and under the care of doctors in medical centers such as St. Louis, which were larger than their small town offered. She sought help from a much loved cousin from her former Forbes community. This was Flora Belle Forbes, known variously as "Flora," "Flo," "Flory," or "Flo Belle." She was a young teacher, known for her skill in handling the students—always a number of them older and larger than she—and for her wide-ranging knowledge. It was said that from her mother's side of the family she inherited the best characteristics and abilities of her doctor grandfather (of the Dutch Loar family), who was also a minister, and her lawyer father. Her strong religious faith and her knowledge of music came from all of the Forbes clan, plus an interest in, and love of, literature that never wavered. She was a little person, 5'2" in height at most, small boned, and slender, with coal-black, fine curly hair and large, almost black eyes. She served as janitor for her school, building the fire as soon as she arrived each morning, and sweeping the floors at the close of the afternoon session. Her transportation was by horseback, using a lady-like sidesaddle. When Julia asked for help, Flo went from northwest Missouri to Eastern Kansas. It was here that she met Julia's stepson, Tom Lowe. In 1890 they were married.

Typical Oregon Desert Country. Sagebrush Stretched for Miles and Water was Scarce.

CHAPTER TWO

This was the era of the Oklahoma Land rushes. Like many other young couples who wanted land, the Lowes traveled by horse-drawn wagon to the area near Stroud, Oklahoma, where they lived for a few years. Tom served for some time as sheriff, but his innate love was farming, as his father had farmed before him. By this time the farmland in the areas mentioned—in Kansas and Missouri in particular—was quite well parceled out. Also, the farms were bequeathed to the older sons in the families, which left the younger sons with no land. The inevitable happened—more and more individuals and families looked westward. Such was the situation with Tom and Flora Lowe. Both felt the urge to own land, both wanted independence. They now had started a family with the birth of a son, which added an urgency to their desire to establish themselves. Julia Lowe came down to Oklahoma to greet the first child of her stepson and cousin. This child was named "Julian" in her honor. Strangely, the little fellow was born with a "club" foot, so Julia and Flora were faced with a problem that they would have to solve themselves. Julia had to return to Kansas, but Flora devised "splints" for the little foot, and for months faithfully changed them—using pads to prevent chafing and pain—but wrapping them tightly enough to brace and hold the proper shape. At last the foot was straightened, and in the boy's adult life there was no indication of anything ever having been wrong.

Another dangerous experience came their way, one which tested their faith and will-power. A shallow well could frequently be a problem, and might have to be cleaned and deepened. Usually the smallest of the men would be lowered to the bottom, with a bucket which he would fill. This was then drawn to the surface to be emptied. By repeating this process many times, the brackish sometimes smelly shallow water would be removed and finally a small amount of "sweet" water would trickle slowly into the basin-like bottom of the well. It was a tedious job. It produced only a small amount of water, but better than no water at all. In one particularly hot spell, the well had to be cleaned. The smallest adult available was...Flora! She went down the ladder, and stood with her feet in the unpleasant shallow water. She went through the procedure of filling the bucket, over and over, while the men above drew it up for emptying. Gradually, enough water was collected to satisfy the immediate need, and by using great care to avoid waste, the period of slack water was passed. No one could explain what happened next, but Flora became very ill, running a high fever. There was no doctor available. Home remedies did no good. Tom and little Julian were almost desperate. Then a man arrived. He carried a Bible. When he saw Flora, he asked to be allowed to pray with and for her. Tom says, "He laid his hands on her and began a prayer. She relaxed and listened. He continued the prayer, then laid a hand on her forehead. The fever was gone!" From that time on, her recovery was swift. "It was a miracle. If that little old preacher hadn't come to us that day, she wouldn't have lived. He saved her life." Tom told the story many times, and while he was not thought of as a particularly religious man, he demonstrated his faith in this regard. There never was any doubt in his mind as to the power of that prayer.

In spite of the difficulty in traveling, in spite of the slowness in correspondence, and the uncertainty as to delivery, people did keep in touch with each other with surprising certainty and regularity. Perhaps the size of families, and the development of "communities" made it possible for relatives and friends to keep in touch with each other, if only by the well-known "grapevine." Thus it was that "shirt-tail" relatives who had gone to Oregon, sent back word as to their whereabouts and what they were doing, and either urged younger members of their clans to stay in their home states—or to hurry to gather their possessions and "hit the trail" to the new areas in the west. Tom and Flo had Missouri friends who had settled in the Blue Mountain area in the north part of Eastern Oregon, and in the rapidly growing town of Pendleton. The Yates family, the Lights, and Gus Elstrom, who was an early-day carpenter and "developer," were enthusiastic members of the community. Gus knew of Tom's ability as a carpenter, and sent word to him to leave Oklahoma and come west. Thus it was that Tom and his little family loaded as much of their possessions as they could into a railroad freight car and set out for a lumber camp near the top of the Blue Mountains, stopping first at LaGrande where they reloaded from train to lumber wagon, going up through Hilgard, and Meacham along the Grande Ronde River to the "summit." Tom was hired immediately to work at preparing lumber for the Pendleton trade. Flora cooked for sections of the workmen, and in spite of having walked for miles beside the lumber wagon from LaGrande, or having ridden part of the way over the bumpy rocky stretches, was in good health. She looked again to the birth of a baby, this time in October. Julian, at his father's heels, was an interested spectator of the logging processes. Mr. and Mrs. Yates, when they learned of Flora's pregnancy, insisted that the couple should go down the mountains to Pendleton, away from the snow and ice of expected winter, that Tom should build, buy, or rent a small house near a grade school for Julian, and obtain a doctor for Flora when her time came.

When the Lowes—Tom, Flora and Julian, came down from the Blue Mountains to Pendleton, their chief goal was to find a satisfactory location where they could build or rent a small house before the birth of their second child. Pendleton was beginning to grow and one of the most interesting building areas was on the hill near the high school. Some of the homes were large, some small and neat and many were middle-sized. It looked promising. They bought a nice lot diagonally across from the school building and Tom promptly bought material for building a house. He divided his days between the company for which he had worked in the mountains, for which he continued to work in town, and on the building project for his own home. However, the second child, a girl, was born in October before the house was completed. This caused an increase in the speed used on the work being done on the house and almost before he could realize it, the finishing touches were being put on.

It was a snug and well-built, medium-sized house and each member of the household was pleased with some particular feature. Tom liked the size of the porch and the area built for tools. Flora liked the large kitchen, the parlor with space for a sofa and for the upright piano. Each person had a special reason to like the library with its rows and rows of books. Even the baby soon liked the low shelves with calico-paged picture books. Julian liked the space for crayons, black ink and pens and drawing paper. These he used to illustrate Longfellow's "Hiawatha," which he was reading in school. There were four bedrooms in the house and a separate bathroom and toilet which was a matter of much pride!

For some reason, the completion of the house marked a change in nomenclature. Very few people used the familiar "Tom" and "Flo" or "Flora." Now, *Mr. and Mrs. Lowe* lived here! Nothing had been said about this change—it just happened. Mr. and Mrs. Colesworthy lived in a gracious home across the street and the two women found much to talk about in the field of education. Mrs. Colesworthy's sister, Miss Rosina Epple, was one of the outstanding, perhaps the first, of primary teachers in the state of Oregon who used the "sound" system (phonics) instead of the old time "A-B-AB" method of teaching reading. The Raymonds lived about a block away and their second daughter Jessie, in spite of the difference in age, spent hours in the Lowe's kitchen talking to Mrs. Lowe about music. The Salings lived a short distance in the other direction and in addition to their older children had a boy about the age of the Lowe's baby girl (who was known as 'Babe'.)

One of the very interesting couples nearby was Mr. and Mrs. Fred Lockley. Mr. Lockley was associated with *The Pendleton East Oregonian,* and later with the *Portland Oregonian* where he made quite a name for himself as editor and as a free-lance writer. When the two Mrs. L's (Lowe and Lockley) were friends in Pendleton, Mrs. Lockley one day let it be known that she thought that a 3-year-old girl child who was talking and using quite a vocabulary, was old enough to have a real name—not just "Babe." Mrs. Lowe explained that she and her husband had planned to name the baby for her grandmother, Huldah Loar Forbes, but Mr. Lowe was not really happy about the choice and "Babe" had been the temporary compromise. Mrs. Lockley remarked, "She looks just like her father. Does he have a name other than 'Tom'?" when she heard "Thomas Marion," she said immediately, "THERE's your name! I'm surprised that you didn't realize it sooner! But use the feminine spelling, 'Marian.' If you want to honor her grandmother, use 'Huldah,' also." Unfortunately the combination became "Huldah Marian" instead of "Marian Huldah," so it was always necessary to explain that "Huldah" WAS "Marian," and that was me! At least I had a name, although it had required three years to accomplish! The naming was none too soon, for in the summer months before my fifth birthday a name became a necessity.

In the first year after the new home was completed, my family learned that their chosen location had a utilitarian possibility. Papa had no desire to return to the top of the Blue Mountains. Nor was he much pleased with the 'development' of Pendleton which was moving slowly. His mind turned again and again to his first love—a farm somewhere with rich soil and a climate with sufficient rainfall or other available water. He began exploring the outlying areas of Pendleton and found much of interest, but not completely to his liking. The wheat ranch type of farming was very different from the Kansas, Missouri and Oklahoma farming areas that he remembered. It was a shock to him to learn that the majority of the high school age students had to leave their homes to come a considerable distance into town if they were to continue past the eighth grade. No cars were available in those days. Some students found jobs with "room and board" available, but it was a "tight" situation for all concerned. Father discovered also that a general caretaker was needed at the high school. This included all kinds of work from small repairing jobs to janitoring. He took the job.

Mama unexpectedly found youngsters from the outlying farms—and their parents—at her door asking if they might eat the noon meal or evening supper with her, or whatever or whenever she would prepare for them. There were more jobs available for boys than for girls, particularly if at least one meal could be located (no 'quickie) foods in those days!) and the Lowes' home had high recommendations. Thus began a procession of young people who, fascinated by the library and its reference books and by my mother's caring and intelligent conversations, came to spend more and more time in the household when jobs did not require after school time to earn enough money for a bedroom somewhere. (One of the boys slept at night in the local funeral parlor.) Had my mother and father not "put the foot down" they might have been managing a restaurant and rooming house with attached supervised study room! Many an English "theme" was written in that library; many an act from Shakespeare read aloud and many lines of Latin translated. The benefit was not a one-way affair. We two Lowe children, Julian of mid-grade school age, and I, always fascinated listener of stories (fables, history, ballads or Bible) learned much more than the high school visitors realized. Geographical names became commonplace to me. Two or three of the not-quite-fourteen year old boys who were in Latin class taught me to repeat: "Mica, mica parva stella," and the succeeding three lines with the advice that, "If you know 'Twinkle, twinkle, little star,' (who didn't), you know what 'Mica, mica, parva stella' means." It worked! Probably, it was due to what the educator Noel McInnis called "The magic of human interaction."

Inevitably, one or two high school girls were drawn into the group and a few more parents could breathe a sigh of relief at having a wholesome influence for their daughters who now were able to attend high school. Jessie Raymond's family lived in their huge home only a block away, but she was allowed to spend much time at our house because her parents were pleased with the influence of my mother and the healthy effect on her grades! Jessie had skill at the piano and her pretty clothes and jewelry were fascinating to me. Jessie remained a close friend to the family for as long as she lived.

Delva St. Clair came from a family from Massachusetts where her father had operated a store. He bought a wheat ranch but his fragile health failed and death soon followed. Delva was determined to graduate from high school and to become a teacher. Her mother married again, so Delva was free to make the Lowes' home HER home. There never was a legal bond completed, but she was always called a "foster sister." If we moved, she moved with us. She was married from our home. Her children called Mama and Papa "Grandma" and "Grandpa" and anniversaries and Christmases were celebrated together. No sister could have been closer or dearer to us and both happy times and sad ones were shared as the years went by.

At the time we lived there, a Mr. Landers and a Mr. Conklin were in the administrative section of the Pendleton schools. Like Tom Lowe, Mr. Conklin longed to live on a farm and it was not long before he was telling Papa that he had a farm in southeastern Oregon, two or three miles out of Ontario in the small Cairo district and was going to enter the Ontario school administration offices. He wanted Papa to move to Ontario, rent the Conklin farm and live in the second house, which was near the Conklin house. Before a decision was reached and any change of location made, nearly a year passed. After school was over in the spring of 1905, Mr. Landers made friends with me as he walked to the high school on his way past our home. I appeared to be older than I was and, due to the association with the students in my home, I had acquired quite a vocabulary. Mr. Landers asked my mother if he might enroll me in the Field grade school the coming Fall, but when he learned that I was not yet four years of age, he dropped the subject!

That fall, Mama attended her first and last football game. Among the boys who spent time in our library was one who was a considerably better-than-average football player. His name was George Strand. He later became prominent in the management of what was to become the famous Pendleton Round Up. He convinced Mama that she should see at least one football game—else how could she discuss the matter with any intelligence? One of the women in the original Missouri group who had come to Pendleton shortly before my parents, had just received a stunning new rubber-tired buggy, at about the time when Pendleton High School was to play football with Baker High School. A handsome horse drew the buggy. The two women were to bring me and go to see the game.

Mama's opinion of the game has never been known in its fullest expression When the game was over and the crowd was leaving, suddenly, very close to the horse and buggy, the band struck up! The horse reared, whirled and bolted, and set off down the street at a terrific pace with the buggy swinging and swaying behind. Before long some of the men in the crowd caught hold of the horse's bridle and at length brought him to a stop, but not until the women had been thrown from the buggy, the driver clutching the reins as well as she could, and my mother clutching her little girl—me—using her own body to form a shield between me and the roadway. In some unknown way, I became wrapped in the farthest length of the reins and rolled for a considerable distance, surviving with nothing more serious than a skinned finger! But Mama's body and especially her face, as she tried to cover my face, received the full impact of her fall. Her face was badly torn, especially her nose, and for most of her life she bore scars as mementoes of her trip to her first football game!

In the next summer before my fifth birthday which was in October, the question of my starting to school in September arose again and I was enrolled. By this time a rotating paper-covered world globe had been added to the reference materials in the library, and I had been taught by some of the students to recognize the proper colors for oceans (I didn't know what they were!) and for the area of the western hemisphere that indicated roughly the western states and rivers—especially the Umatilla and the Columbia—and at last, "Here's where I live!" although it surely was an inexact bit of locating. It did not carry much meaning to this young geographer, except that I loved the sounds of the various names.

It seemed only a very short time until Miss Epple's first-grade class was "sounding out" a good number of words, and as the days went by it seemed as though a key had been laid into these eager hands, with the promise that more and more doors would be unlocked as new or different "readers" were placed in them.

The Teachers' Institute was to be held in the "opera house" or auditorium in Pendleton that first fall, and Miss Epple's class was to demonstrate what was being done by the use of the "sound system." The class was lined up on the stage and various words were suggested from those in attendance and written on the blackboard. The children were to 'sound' the words to themselves and hold up a hand if they thought they knew the word. After a few short words a longer one was written. There was silence. Mothers had been invited for that afternoon session, but the children were oblivious to everything except the board and the strange-looking word. Suddenly, I knew the word! Up went the hand. Miss Epple hesitated, then explained to the audience that there was a letter combination that had not previously been shown the class so this was hardly a proper test for them.

My hand began to wave. Mama was distressed. She doubted that I knew the word and she did not want me to be marked as a failure on my first appearance as a school child! I continued to wave my hand. "Why, oh *why*, doesn't Miss Epple call on me before someone else says the word?" I knew the word. I KNEW, *I KNEW*! Someone on the stage said, "Why not let the little one try? She thinks she knows!" So Miss Epple explained that this "little one" was younger than the others—the word was new, but..."Marian, would you like...?" No more was needed! "COLUMBIA!" I almost shouted. Mama took a breath. The audience clapped. After the meeting, at home, I asked, "Why did they clap?" Mama explained that the applause had been for Miss Epple and the whole class, and I said, "That was nice." Mama said, "Yes, Miss Epple *is* a *teacher*!" So, we might say, were the high school students at the Lowe's who had spoken of the Columbia!

In the winter that followed this first experience at school, my parents sold their house, packed all of their household belongings, including the piano and the books, in a railroad freight car and made the trip back over the blue Mountains down along the lovely Grande Ronde River, to La Grande-Baker, Huntington, and Ontario, and to the home on the Conklin farm. Mr. Conklin drove a horse and buggy from the farm to the Ontario school, taking his children and Julian and me. Julian transferred from the Pendleton school district without trouble, but I had some difficulty, for I had no arithmetic in the brief time I spent in the Field school, and I had been placed in the third grade in the Ontario school, because I could read at that level. But arithmetic was something else, as was penmanship. One of the boys and I occasionally were sent to the blackboard to practice writing a sentence. Eddie wrote uphill and I wrote downhill and the boys and girls in the class laughed at both of us. Oh...misery! Mama and Papa realized that I was out of my depth in a third grade class, so took me from the Ontario school and entered me in the Cairo country school, approximately one mile from our home. This was an excellent solution. I read with those who read at my level, regardless of age. The teacher introduced me to the "2x's" and "3x's" ("two-tums" and "three-tums") and my ex-teacher-mother explained what was involved so I understood the issues, and merely had to work on considerable memorizing to speed the proceedings. The teacher was acquainted with all of us students—and we all knew each other. On Sundays there was a Sunday school in the school building where there were occasional little programs which we enjoyed—except when Roscoe Conklin and I had to sing, "Jesus bids us shine with a clear, pure light, Like a little candle shining in the night... ." We each carried a candle, and we wore a night shirt and a nightgown, respectively. Mercifully, the boys and girls did not laugh at us!

One of the joys of recess time at Cairo was when we laid some crossed pins on the railroad track, which was very close to the schoolhouse; then waited happily for the train to come by to or from Vale, the County Seat. After which noisy event, at the next recess or noon, we would go out to collect our miniature "scissors." Strange to say, the teacher and our parents took a dim view of this happy scissor-making project!

CHAPTER 3

The years at Cairo were satisfactory in many ways, but the more pleased the people concerned found themselves, the more serious the problems that did arise. Papa liked the "lay of the land"...the way it could be irrigated. He liked the type of soil; his appetite was whetted for land of his own. He found almost no farms for sale and the prices seemed high for him and Mama, if they *did* succeed in finding an available place. On the Conklin farm they saw their first sugar beets. They were seeded, weeded, thinned, topped and at last loaded on the freight cars to be taken to the sugar factory. Also nearly every farm had a small orchard or at least a few fruit trees. There were barns for the cattle and horses. On such a farm a family could grow together and develop a sense of solidarity. Here family customs might originate and mature, as did one involving Mama and me.

By the time of my birthday in October of our first year in Cairo, practically all of the trees were bare of fruit and the leaves were thick on the ground. Mama and I walked together along the rows of barren trees, when suddenly my foot shoved some of the leaves to one side, and there lay a lovely plump pear! Mama explained how it would have to be tucked away in a dark place for a while but promised that we would come back to get it at the right time...and a tradition was born! From that time until the time of her death, Mama and I "observed" my birthday together although we might be physically far apart. If we were together, we went for a walk. If either of us was in a location where she might go for a walk, but not we two together, the walk was made by each alone; but if we realized that going for a walk would be an impossibility for both because of travel, school (college), or for whatever reason, then we resorted to the mail. It was "fair" to write, either on the birthday or before it, or if for some reason it was necessary, a letter could be written a day late. However, through all the years, there was a special tie between us which was strengthened at each of my birthdays.

Then came Papa's opportunity! New sagebrush land was opened for homesteading! Papa heard reports on this land, its general contour, richness, distance from Nyssa, Vale, Parma and the communities lying approximately the same distance from each. He saw the network of rivers, principally the Snake and the Owyhee, plus the irrigation system, watering the Owyhee farms already under the "old ditch," a system that would water all of the land newly opened for homesteading. When he personally inspected the area his knowledge of how to "find the corners" of the land and his skill in carpentry stood him in good stead. In his mind's eye he could see where the corner posts of his fields would be and how close to the southern line of the 160 acres he should build a house in order to waste none of the farmland, yet leave plenty of room for future barns, feed lots, haystacks and corrals. He knew he was looking far, far into the future, but "Hope springs eternal..."

"Hillway Homestead," with Marian, Age 7 and her Dog, Sailor, in Foreground. The Tent at Right Housed an Extra Hired Man or a Guest. At Far Right is the Old Buggy. In this Picture, the Homestead House was Sided with Tarpaper, Which was Common at that Time.

If Papa was busy—so too was Mama, and the "busy-ness" began immediately upon the arrival of the first wagon load of household necessities at the homestead and continued through the unloading of the piano, plus the grain sacks and gunny sacks stuffed with magazines, the set of Encyclopedia Britannica, sets of readers, from Cyr's First to the Fifth, and spellers and one or two elementary geographies; likewise one or two arithmetics which included an elementary and middle-grade edition (this for Julian's special use.) There were copies of the classics and of some of the well-known works of American writers—among them Longfellow's, which must have had a definite effect on Julian; who was old enough to write a brief theme on the responsibilities of husband and wife as taught in the Hiawatha stories in the "Song of Hiawatha" (Hiawatha's Wooing.) Cooperation and mutual help was the theme. The lilt and rhythm of the poetry stayed with both children and was a joy through many years, especially when Delva came from Pendleton High School and made it part of her contribution to the family life to read aloud whenever the occasion arose. The fact that she could not "carry a tune" was of no consequence when she read so beautifully. Who could forget..."The sun says, 'Love is sunshine, hate is shadow. Life is checkered shade and sunshine; Rule by love, O Hiawatha.' The Moon says, "...Day is restless, night is quiet, ...Rule by patience, Laughing Water'."

The advice given in the poem hardly matches the modern hard-won independence of women, in which struggle the state of Oregon was then in the forefront. Mama's friend Mrs. Ivanhoe of La Grande was the first woman county school superintendent in Oregon. A few years later than Mrs. Ivanhoe's era a young woman, a graduate of the University of Oregon in Eugene, small, intelligent, "dressy," with long beautiful red hair piled high on her head was appointed by the "powers that be" in county government in Vale, Oregon, to become the county school superintendent for Malheur County. This was Fay Clark, whose path as superintendent of schools inevitably led her to Mama. A long and mutually productive and enjoyable association followed. However, before a close personal friendship had time to ripen, there were a number of events that followed those years at "Hillway Homestead" as Mama always called it. Mama's interest in people was always in the forefront. In the first few months of our life at Hillway the head man of a group of surveyors, whose camp was about a mile away, came to get acquainted. It was soon apparent that he was a man of integrity and of learning. He read excerpts to Mama from letters from his mother in the east. One of them was a quotation from "Each In His Own Tongue", by William Herbert Carruth. Although it carried rather mature phraseology for the children, the repetition of "...others call it God," was full of meaning and beauty. When the surveyors were preparing to leave the area, this same leader of the group arrived for a farewell visit. In his hand he carried a very small packet for Mama. It was a little blue-gray booklet containing the four stanzas of "Each in His Own Tongue." He had asked his mother to sent it for Mama. For years it occupied a small, but important place on the shelf just above the library table. Many people came to visit with us at Hillway, and it seemed that each person had something of himself to contribute to our way of life, to our thinking, or both.

When we lived in Pendleton the family enjoyed good health except for one unpleasant problem. About once a year I experienced a very painful earache. The first year in Cairo near Ontario started well healthwise, but before the winter was over the earache struck again. It was the worst one thus far, with swelling inside the main portion of the ear. A phone call to the doctor brought information as to how to make and use poultices to encourage the swelling to "break." This was the most painful of the various earaches I had had. The curls on the ear-ache-side of my head had been cut off, to allow room for poulticing. Some time after our arrival at Hillway, before the hair had time to grow back again, Mama's cousin Daisy from Missouri came to Eastern Oregon, probably to Nyssa, and was brought out to Hillway Homestead for a visit. Immediately after the first greeting, she drew back, took a long look at me, laid a hand on my shoulder and said, "Flory...Marian...what do we have *here*?" Mama made a brief explanation, after which Cousin Daisy said to me one of the nicest, most reassuring things that I remembered having heard. She said, "Now, remember this: we will *never* have another earache. This was the *last one*!" Imagine the joy from that statement! No more of the excruciating pain. From that day to this I have had *no* earache. It was another miracle!

Not long after Cousin Daisy's visit, Papa and Mama undertook some changes in our way of living, at least in regard to the size and shape of our homestead house. Both realized that without doubt we would need more sleeping arrangements for the numerous visitors, and for the relatives who had already begun to arrive...usually without warning. A one-room house could pose serious problems for more than two or three inhabitants, and certainly demanded ingenious arrangments. A curtain across one end of the main room offered privacy for the double bed area that belonged to Papa and Mama. A rather well-worn, medium-sized velveteen sofa at a right angle to their bed and in front of a window, provided a bed for me—unless I could persuade the "folks" to let me sleep in the narrow little attic above their bed. This was reached by a ladder fastened to the wall nearby. Julian usually claimed this space when he was at home instead of staying overnight in the home of someone for whom he was working. How well I remember the music of the occasional rain storms that beat down on the shingled attic roof! The only other sound that rivaled that of the rain was the howling of the coyotes. If the rainstorms were music, the coyotes' calls were symphonies...in which our half-breed dog joined joyously! Papa and Mama always reminded me to listen to the answers that the coyotes made to each other back and forth...the mature calls interspersed with young "yip-yip-yurr-r-r's!"

Our house must have been very crowded. In addition to the sleeping arrangements there was a good-sized extendable dining room table in the room, and of course a cookstove, plus a shelf of books and the upright piano. with the "breaking" of the sagebrush (a process of actually breaking down the bushes with horse-drawn implements) and raking and burning it, the plowing, harrowing, leveling, and seeding for the first crop of rye began. The dust flew! Sometimes whirl-winds swept across the land and into the house, leaving layers of dust on every piece of furniture or convenient ledge. The books and the piano had to be kept covered. The covers that were used were large sheets of a dark material that were lined with a type of fleecy cloth. We all endured these covers but detested them. We knew that the piano, especially had to be covered, unless we were sure that "company" was coming, when some one of us would shake the cover outdoors. Perhaps our vocal protestations precipitated the proceedings that took our breath away (Julian's and mine), but more probably fate stepped in, in the guise of a real need of a "cash-flow;" for one day the piano and the prized set of encyclopedias were loaded into a wagon and carried away. In exchange for them Papa brought from the purchaser a two or three volume set of an encyclopedia which, as the years went by, we probably used more than we would have used the classical and erudite multi-volumned "Britannica," had we kept it. The substitute for the piano was at first very difficult to accept and to learn to use, but before too long it became almost like a plaything, as well as a challenge. It was a "reed-organ" with "stops" to punch or to pull, in any of many combinations, from very soft sounds to very loud. It had "couplers" to make additional octaves. It had knee bellows, and its full sound was made by pedals which were worked alternately by the feet. At first it was very difficult to use one's feet and at the same time one's fingers; but little by little, after much practice, it became a pleasure. Still the house was too small but Papa got out his trusty tool cabinet and almost before we knew what he had planned, an addition to the back side of the house began to take shape. It extended the full length of the house, with two rooms; one, a kitchen that was behind the then-present cook stove and dining area, and the other, a bedroom behind Papa and Mama's room. Mama and Papa were clever in arranging shelves and cupboards and spaces for hanging clothes. In some corners Papa put a sturdy triangular-shaped shelf, with a rod beneath it where clothes hangers could be placed. A curtain in front hid all of the hangers and clothes and made a neat pseudo-closet. Although many different people used the room, we always thought of it as "Delva's room."

By the time these changes were completed we had become acquainted with our nearest neighbors, one mile to the south. To reach their house we had to go through sagebrush land, to their orchard and farmland that lay "below the big ditch" (meaning that those areas were irrigated from the water in the big ditch which, in turn, received its water from a reservoir back of a dirt, rock and brush dam on the Owyhee River beyond Mitchell Butte.) This ditch for its "day and age" was truly a *big* ditch. Papa and Mama were told that it carried water for 10,000 acres of land, from its beginning at the dam to the point where it spilled into the Snake River. If a man's property had too much elevation to irrigate from this gravity ditch, he could, under certain circumstances, use a water wheel, a gas engine, or some other device to run water from the ditch to a spot on his land where gravity could take over. Hence the descriptive words for certain lands were "above the ditch" or "below the ditch." These nearest neighbors were Charley and Belle Bradley. They had a beautiful little girl named Ruby, and I was fascinated by her. Later on they had another little girl, Alta, who also was a lovely little one. I can remember seeing her in her "jumper." Charley's parents lived here also and later on his mother, known to all as "Grandma Bradley" lived in a little new house very close to Charley and Belle.

The Bradley orchard was an adventure for anyone, but especially to people like us, who had *no* trees! There were many kinds of fruit, including several varieties of apples. The Bradleys had a big garden. Thus we had a source of fruit and vegetables, and even of water from their well before we had one of our own. Papa hauled the water in a barrel placed on runners and pulled by one or two of our horses. We now had a faithful older horse who was a "jack of all trades." He was a quarter-horse who was supposed to have belonged to Bill Hanley, well-known cattleman of the

Burns area, and to have been an excellent cattle worker before he became too old. I learned to ride him and found him smart and obedient. Imagine my happiness when I learned that a gentle kick in the side from my bare heel would send him into a special gait! He was a "single-footer." He was the horse that we used to pull the red cart that was our means of conveyance unless Papa hitched a team to the spring-wagon. "Prince" was a horse that was easy to saddle or bridle, or to put the harness on for the cart. He would accept a surcingle, or even a sidesaddle, which was a saddle used only rarely because few people owned one. A sidesaddle was a relic, and a reminder of life in the parts of the states of Missouri and Kansas that Papa and Mama remembered.

Mama had ridden her mare "sidesaddle" to and from the school where she first taught, occasionally having to urge the mare to swim if a sudden freshet obliterated the road and changed the stream banks into precipitous approaches that forced the mare to scramble for footing. She was a small horse, "a woman's horse" and Mama was a good rider. Mama always "stood up for the underdog" as the saying went, and her wrath was stirred whenever her younger, but much larger, brother saddled the little mare with a man's full saddle and galloped away to whatever destination he had in mind. I knew that Julian *never* would have done such a thing! My father would not have allowed it! But, chiefly, Julian was like Mama. He "looked out for" other people's rights including mine, and Delva's whenever she was with us, although she was about as much older than he was, as he was older than "Sis" (meaning me.)

A visit one evening to our neighbors about a mile away from us to the west set the stage for a never-forgotten experience. Lem and "Izzy" Wilson and their young family were dry-land homesteaders like we were, but they had a good well. Lem proved to be eager to branch out as a well-driller. He had a good supply of drilling apparatus and before the evening was over, he and Papa had made an agreement to work together. We had driven to the Wilson's in the spring wagon that night and how glad we were that we had, as there was nothing to obstruct our view in any direction or overhead. On the way home about halfway to our Hillway Homestead, the sky lit up as though with dazzling fireworks shooting in all directions but chiefly upward and forward, seeming to be led by one terrific leading star, if star it was! We had known of "falling stars" but never of anything like this! We stopped the wagon and gazed spellbound. This was 1910, and we were witnessing Halley's Comet on a return visit from its last appearance in 1759! How Papa and Mama knew what they were seeing, I do not know, but already the magazines and newspapers that were to be hallmarks of our home wherever that home might be, were beginning to arrive, so I suppose that the folks must have read of the expected comet when they were catching up on the news. Perhaps they read of it by lamp light in the evening after dinner when Papa was home from working for someone, somewhere, and we were celebrating a "Cotter's Saturday Night"* to which we had looked forward all week. Mama's handsome, red, glass fruit holder was lined with quarters of apples and filled with what would have been "peanut brittle" candy in more affluent surroundings, but was a variation of that with us, due to the absence of any kind of nuts, but made palatable by the addition of what to us was a very new kind of dry breakfast food, bought to use only for making this variety of candy. It was called "Puffed Rice!"

The Spring Wagon from which the Lowes saw the Spectacular Halley's Comet in 1910

Mama believed in taking advantage of every new situation that came our way, saying that since we were so far away from larger centers of civilization, we should be aware of, and learn from any of those situations whenever opportunity brought them our way. Sometimes the results were amazing, sometimes amusing, most of the time they were unexpected. Attendance at the Owyhee School was on a basis of being there if you wanted to be, or, for the larger boys and girls, attendance might depend on how much the parents needed the children to help with farm work at

* From poet Bobby Burns' reference to the hard-working Scotsman who has returned home and is relaxing on the weekend.

special times, for instance, at harvesting. So, one spring day I was at school when Julian was not. About half way through the afternoon one or two of the pupils suddenly said, "Oh, look!" When the teacher looked, too, she told us that all of us could look out of the windows and what a surprise met our eyes! Coming on the road toward the school house was A CAR! I doubt that any of us had actually seen one before. Certainly there were no cars anywhere in the community. But, possibly with the memory of a picture that we had seen somewhere and probably with our memory reinforced by the teacher's statement that, "Yes, that IS a car!" we said in unison, "A CAR!" It came to the hitching area in front of the schoolhouse, and stopped. Two men came to the front door. Now we could get a good look at the vehicle, which was red, had no top, but had one wide front seat. One of the men asked the teacher if Marian Lowe was there. He presented a letter stating that he and his friend were going to the Lowes' homestead and they (the Lowe's) hereby gave permission for Marian to leave school before four o'clock and ride home in the car!! Of all of the breath-taking experiences in my life, I think this was the prize. The men had wanted to talk to Papa about a possible land purchase and when Mama heard Papa say that he knew one of them owned a car, the whole idea of arranging my ride came into her mind. That was typical of Mama! Some time after this event, Mama received a letter from one of her women-cousins in Missouri who had never "been west." The cousin concluded her letter with a loving plea, "Oh, Flory, please do come back home. Come out of that wild country. You and the whole family may be killed by Indians!" We knew the cousin was serious and well-meaning, but what a laugh we had! If the Owyhee neighborhood had once upon a time been "wild country" it was far from that now. One of us had even had a ride in a car! As for the Indians, we hadn't seen one since we left Pendleton where the handsome Umatillas were seen on the streets, singly or in groups. It was a common sight and they were friendly to all. True, that there once had been Indians in our area—we knew from finding arrowheads. These were in many sizes, and from gleaming black flint to almost white rock of many varieties. As the farms were developed the arrowheads disappeared, often being plowed under.

One year Mama spent most of her time in teaching—and I was the pupil! Papa and Julian were working on farms "below the ditch" and Mama had no desire to see her daughter growing up without schooling.

Papa and Mama thought the two and one-half to three mile walk to the Owyhee schoolhouse was too far for me alone, so Papa built a blackboard for me. It was on an easel, wide enough for arithmetic problems, spelling lessons, and primitive maps, among other types of school work. There was an eraser rack, of which I was very proud. Mama had boxes of chalk to be used carefully, avoiding careless breakages. As a change of pace from ordinary school subjects, Mama taught me to read music, and we both were delighted when I mastered a simple march tune. To be sure that I understood march rhythm, Mama marched around the room while I played the organ and when I'd miss a note or break the rhythm she would stop, stand on one foot and pretend to stagger until I could get the march-time established, so she could march again. From the first simple march it was an easy step to "Love Divine, All Loves Excelling" which was the first hymn that I played at Sunday School, one Sunday when the regular organist was absent. I was much embarrassed when I was asked to play another hymn, for "Love Divine" was my only hymn! The kindly superintendent said, "That's all right, Marian. Whenever you have other hymns that you can play, you just let me know, and we'll sing *them*." It was a tremendous incentive to me. I found that hymns in the key of "C" or with no more than one flat were easier for me than others, so I devised a simple procedure to learn them. I would go through the *Pentecostal Hymns, Numbers One and Two* (or whatever numbers we had) and work on the hymns that were written in those keys. That gave me quite a number of possibilities. I'm not sure that they were always the most appropriate ones for the particular Sunday's lesson, but with basic Bible teaching, most of the gospel and evangelistic hymns were safe choices! These were my "stock in trade" while I worked on more and more that I had not played before. Bless those understanding people! In later years, I was to bless them even more as my ability to "sight read" developed. Thus, the period of "Mama-Marian" schooling began to bear fruit.

The Hack, a Larger Buggy, to Accommodate all Four of the Lowes

(L. to R.) Marian Lowe, Mrs. Lowe, Delva St. Clair, and a School Friend of Ma
(Note the Exciting Hats!)
1912

Owyhee Dam—Ring-gate Spillway Showing Forms Before the Concrete was Poured

The Upper Dam (Looking Downstream)
This Dam Provided Irrigation Water to 100,000 Acres of Desert Country
The First Sagebrush Dam Watered 10,000 Acres

The Owyhee Dam—Forerunner of the Columbia Dam
Here Workers Were Experimenting with Grouting and Freezing on the Lower Side

AIR, SUNLIGHT AND A BIT OF LAND

CHAPTER 4

Homesteading was a "far cry" from having an irrigated farm as Papa had wanted, but having a farm meant having irrigation water, and as yet that was impossible. Delva was now old enough to file for land in her name, but suitable land was hard to find. Papa and Mama learned that in some few areas not too far away from Hillway there were locations for "squatters" claims. One of these was in the bowl-shaped area south of Mitchell Butte and a short distance, perhaps half a mile or less, from the hot spring on the low end of the butte. Surprisingly enough, most of the land in the "bowl" had been withdrawn from homesteading because there was a slight possibility that it might be wanted for a reservoir back of a dam near the butte. However, Jake Huffman had an improved farm adjoining the outer edge of the bowl, on the side flanked by the Owyhee River. A water wheel lifted the water. Most people felt *that* farm surely would not be taken as part of the reservoir site, so if a person was willing to take a chance on Squatters' Rights on unclaimed land, he/she might not be evicted. There were a few other people in the bowl, but the Huffmans were the only ones whose farm had some useable products. Mrs. Huffman, for instance, who had lived on the farm for many, many years, was the first person to have asparagus, which was sometimes called "fire grass."

Anyway, Papa, Mama, and Delva decided that she should file "Squatters' Rights" in the bowl. Since it wasn't considered proper for a young woman to live alone on a claim, I was the companion for her while she lived in the small one-room house that Papa built for her. We carried water from the Owyhee Ditch for mopping the floor. We carried good drinking water from a well on the land owned by another member of the Huffman family, and we walked to the hot spring carrying a wash basin to use in washing our hair in the wonderful "soft" water outside the primitive little bath house that housed the main flow. Soap was not to be used in the bath house because it created a lather that could be cleaned out only with great labor. But what a thrill it was to soak one's self in the hot water! Papa would always open the lower end of the bath pool after it had been used and would direct a new flow of fresh hot water into the "tub."

Instead of my being a companion for Delva, she was a fascinating companion for me. Papa and Mama always provided food for us,

A Tunnel at the Owyhee Dam
The Walls are Cut through Basalt Rock

sometimes cooked (for the first few days of our stay) or dried, or canned. From these provisions Delva would prepare what I thought were delicious meals. My favorite was cottage-fried potatoes with a can of tomatoes! Delva varied the menu whenever she could, but I always begged for the same thing! The most fascinating time of the day came in the evening when Delva could be cajoled into telling stories, or better yet, into reciting poetry, preferably ballads, usually based on some phase of Indian life or legends. These ballads had the rhythm and general themes of Longfellow's poems, but were adapted to life in the Oregon Territory. It was wonderful to listen to Delva's musical voice while the story unfolded and to listen for the natural accompaniments like the ripple of the Owyhee River across the rocks where the river narrowed in the canyon above us. Near the dam that impounded the water for the Owyhee Ditch, but across the river, there were semi-circular high banks, their contour resembling the tooth-marks of a giant comb, and from which some beautiful echoes could be heard along with the lonesome, musical questioning "Hoo-hoo?" of the little hoot-owls who lived nearby.

Papa's desire to have a real farm instead of Hillway Homestead made him an eager listener when "land promoters" came his way. Canadian wheatland was the lure this time. Supposedly, the land could be purchased for little, and sold for much, so Americans from all over the western states, even from south into California, made up train loads of eager buyers. The land in which Papa was interested was in the province of Alberta. He made the investment, but by the time all of the expenses had been met, such as for mechanical farm apparatus with horses to propel it, seed for planting, and workmen to help with all phases including harvesting, there had been quite an investment. Nevertheless, some of the men from the States made considerable money...some did not.

While Papa was away from the homestead, Julian was to stay with one of the neighboring families in the Owyhee neighborhood, where he was to help with the farm chores after school each day and on the weekends. Mama and I went to Ontario, Oregon, where Mama rented a room with the Hannah family and was granted the right to prepare food for the two of us on a "staggered" schedule with them. I was taken to the grade school, where, after a brief visit with the Principal, I was told to enter the fourth grade. It must have been difficult for the teacher to know where to place me for I had almost no formal day-by-day education. But Mama's teaching must have covered the proper material for I remember no difficulties. I loved the teacher and the stories she read to us after lunch each day. I was fascinated with town life. I liked being able to play with other boys and girls of approximately my own age. I was even invited to a birthday party although I hadn't been in Ontario more than a few weeks! The members of the fourth grade class proved to be willing to accept a stranger in their midst. I loved them all.

After school was out that spring, Mama and I stayed in Ontario until we could return to Hillway Homestead, knowing that Papa would be returning before long. When he did come, it was like having a Cotter's Saturday Night every night for at least a week or longer! Papa seemed glad to have had the Canadian experience, but to be happy to return. He had made some money—not a great deal—but enough to ease the pressure somewhat, and to make possible the purchase of the farm he had thought about for a long time. Two things stood out for him, from this trip. First of all, as he told us, he had learned that any location where a man would get his wagon stuck in the snow on the Fifth of June was no place for him except for this temporary journey, and maybe not even for that! So it was, "Goodbye Calgary and Alberta" for a long, long time. The second experience that he had was that he fell in love with Spokane, Washington, after a "lay-over" on his way home. He brought pictures to us, and souvenirs from a shop on Riverside Avenue. One souvenir was a leather purse with a "burnt-work" saying 'Spokane." He couldn't seem to quit talking about the city. I think I must have inherited his feeling!

At last, after his return from his Canadian trip, Papa found the farm that he wanted, that was available, so he cut the ties with Hillway Homestead by selling it, after he signed the papers for the farm. We moved to the location where we were to spend a good many years. Like all farms, this one had its good points and its poor ones. It had eighty acres which was all that one man could handle well without a lot of help. The soil was a nice sandy loam and with the exception of a small area where the south border broke sharply toward a small pond and the river just beyond, it was quite level. Papa felt that a bit of disc harrowing and some work with a fresno* would make that area even more level. The water for irrigation came directly from the "big ditch" on the north border into our laterals (the main ditches from the "big ditch"), which was a definite

**A form of farming implement similar to a scraper.*

advantage. The waste water that on some farms had to run across some one else's land, on this one ran directly to the pond and the river. There was no danger of those bug-a-boos of irrigated country known as "water fights." There was a moderate sized locust grove. There were red and black raspberries and gooseberries and red and white currants, apple, peach and cherry trees in the bluegrass yard.

Winter at the Old Owyhee Farm (1922) Below the Owyhee Ditch

The Hay Wagon—This was a Common Piece of Farming Equipment Around 1937

Stacking Alfalfa Hay at the Old Farm

A Stack of Sagebrush, Cut for Winter Fuel

But alas and alack! The water in the well which was in a convenient location near the back door, was unusable! It smelled like rotten eggs and tasted worse! Neither the chickens nor any of the animals, small or large, would touch it, so we were back in the painful situation of having to haul water as we had to do in the early days of Hillway Homestead, although this time the need was almost desperate, because of more animals and poultry, as well as farm help and company who needed water. From these first days on for months, Papa hauled water from a deep well about two and one-half miles away, pumping by hand to fill a bucket which he lifted via a short ladder, to the top opening on large, cylindrical, wooded tank wagon which was about the size of the tank wagons used in small towns for fire fighting or street washing. Imagine hauling the buckets and dumping them, after having done a hard day's work! There was no time or money for drilling a well. In addition, there was the problem of where to sink the well so that the same unusable sulphur water source would not be tapped. Imagine if you were a busy farm wife, trying to manage with a bare minimum of water. Every drop was precious! Papa reasoned that when he had a little more time he would have a well-driller, perhaps Lem Wilson, sink one or more test bores...but "time was of the essence." Everything needed to be done at once, so it was a long time before we had a well. When we did get it, it was nice water and was halfway between the living area and the corrals, with an engine to move the busy pump so that pipes carried the water to the houses and cattle and to the kitchen of the house, where it came into the sink through a convenient faucet. What a relief!

One of the greatest assest of the farm was its convenient location. A plank footbridge led across the Owyhe "big ditch" through the sagebrush land above the ditch, to the schoolhouse one-half mile away...close enough so that I could hurry home at noon for lunch. A road that followed the ditch-bank led to intersecting roads to the other farms in the Owyhee Community, or to the Kingman Kolony settlement across the Owyhee River. This was bounded by the Snake River on its other side. About a mile along the ditch bank from our farm was a combination store, post office, and home with roads leading to Nyssa, following about three different routes. One of these followed a straight road which led to the present Owyhee Corners and on to the town. Another followed the ditch-bank most of the way. A third meandered through sagebrush land, connecting with a road from the schoolhouse. Each of these roads had its own characteristics and reasons for use.

The store and post office received supplies and mail via buggy from Nyssa. The store was operated by Ben Matthiessen whose wife was a daughter of Grandma Bradley, therefore a sister of Charlie Bradley. Rhoda Matthiessen was about my age. Her parents owned a phonograph with a goodly supply of cylinder records and Rhoda and I spent hours in their home listening to the finest music of the era including records of Caruso, Alma Gluck and others. I don't know how Rhoda's parents had the patience to endure our playing our favorites over and over again, unless our favorites were also theirs, but how we loved those sessions! Ben and Mattie Matthiessen surely could not realize what life-long pleasure they afforded us. I have never forgotten them, or the music.

Music came into my life from two or three other sources. Julian always seemed to be watching for things to do for "little Sis" and he used some of his hard-earned money to pay for a subscription to *The Etude,* a magazine which provided hours of good reading about the world of music, and contained what normally would have been called "sheet music" had it not been in the magazine. My first real piece of sheet music came from Julian, also. It was called "Wild West" and I proudly played it whenever I was asked. This was the era of "Red Wing" and "Rainbow" which had tremendous popularity. In the first winters on the farm Papa and Mama entranced us in the long evenings by playing some old time "hoe-downs" with Papa playing the "fiddle" by ear, since he read no music, and Mama "chording" on the organ. They taught us how to schottische, and to do the waltz and the polka.

In a short time Julian was beginning to play the family violin, taking lessons from Corinne Maxwell in the Kingman Kolony, and playing in Corinne's "orchestra" which produced really enjoyable music. Dainty little Helen Peck played First Violin in the group which was asked to play all around the county and for all kinds of meetings. The Kolony built a schoolhouse that would accommodate a larger crowd that we had room for in our Owyhee School. At one time there was an attempt to move the county seat from Vale to Ontario, and many of us who were quite young experienced what politics could be like on a practical level. Before the election day had come and the matter was settled, meetings had been held in every community in the county. We attended the one in the Kolony schoolhouse. There were speeches pro and con, and music (the orchestra as well as vocal music.) By the end of the meeting emotion was running high. The representatives from Vale concluded with a tearful song the theme of which was "Vale, our home." Papa said the voters could not resist a plea like that and sure enough, Vale won the election (by not more than a handful of votes, but Papa and Mama said, "One vote is enough to win or lose.") For years, I wondered whether it was the "pro and con" speeches that had the greatest influence, or the tearful plea in the music.

Life on the farm was busy, always. The Vale-Ontario struggle had been a rare change from the regular pace. From early morning to until after nine o'clock in the evening there was work to be done and chores. Mama had incubators and 400 chicks were hatched that first year. There were 40 Indian Runner ducks. There were about 25 turkeys and 100 geese. Each type of poultry had to be fed and cared for in its own particular way, which was different from the procedures used for any other. There were pigs to feed—with butchering and making of lard and soap, as well as curing bacon and ham. There were cows to milk, butter to be made and sold. There were ten-gallon cans of whole milk to be taken each morning to the beginning of the milk truck route. For quite a long time this meant taking the cans in the cart and the route started a few miles down the ditch-bank road to the Stam's farm and dairy, where my friend Sytje lived.

In the winters, farmers frequently allowed bands of sheep to be fed near their haystacks until the time for lambing and shearing was over and the exodus to the interior country began. For the housewives there was often work with wool to be done including "carding" (almost like combing, but more difficult) and sometimes making of "batts" for quilts and comforts, although the nicest grades of wool were usually sent to the Oregon Woolen Mills in Portland. Now, in 1981 Spokane, I still have a comforter (re-covered more than once) made from 100% wool batts from that Owyhee farm.

In the spring when it was time for the sheep to go to the interior a major project was begun, with sheep-herders and faithful dogs much in evidence. There were always baby lambs who were too small or sickly to keep up with the herds. These, called "orphans" or "bummers" were hunted and picked up by farmers in buggies or wagons, or in sacks on the back of a horse. Taking care of them was difficult and time-consuming, a day and night job, as the bleating, hungry little babies had to be fed on a regular schedule, teaching them to take milk from a nippled bottle, not over two tablespoons at a time, every two hours around the clock! This insured a well-formed salable lamb later on, with no "pot-belly."

All summer long, from the earliest asparagus to the last apple or parsnip, there were fruits and vegetables to can or dry. There were jams, preserves and jellies to be made, the latter frequently put up in one-gallon cans (at our house.) Pickles of many kinds, sometimes in crocks with grape leaves between their layers to help preserve their color, were stored in an outdoor cellar. Here the telephones came into their own (at one time with about 14 subscribers on one line.) How wonderful it was to have a "phone!" It served many purposes. In the food processing periods housewives traded recipes via phone and kept in touch with each other as to when various kinds of produce were ready for preparation for winter. This trading of recipes was marvelous. One fall season Emma Peutz taught Mama to make "Sauer Gans" which even I (no milk-drinking, no poultry- or egg-eating person) found to be very good!

Charley and Belle Bradley had perhaps the largest number of varieties of fruits in any orchard, and many were the recipes for "goodies" that they shared with others. The Moreys, who were our closest neighbors, had a large orchard too, and in addition had many bee-hives, which made for an ideal combination of fruit blossoms and hungry bees for the production of a delightful creamy white comb-honey. "Scraping honey" (removing unwanted wax from the combs without breaking the tender wax "pockets" and allowing the tasty liquid honey to be wasted) was one of the sources of income for nimble-fingered offspring of various families, usually girls, who learned to avoid, or to suffer bravely, from a few painful and itchy bee stings along the way! When it came to cucumber pickles, Si and Gertie Bigelow had the finest cucumbers, watered faithfully, of uniform size and picked about every second or third day, except when ripe ones were needed for a special pickle. Gertie's ripe cucumber pickles were very special!

Prince, our old "cow pony" had been retired from regular jobs and his place taken by Dandelion, known as an "Arabian buck," with her buckskin-colored hide, set off with long black wavy mane and full length black tail, black forelocks and fetlocks, and a black stripe all the way from her shoulders down her back to her tail. She had the appearance and temperament of a 100% Arabian, needing no whip—ever—nothing to urge her to more speed except through "communication" from the reins. Even the sound of a rein-slap on some other horse in a team would cause her to make a slight jump. When she and I went to Bigelow's for cucumbers she would take a fast dainty trot down the road, but when we returned home with our load of cukes tied behind the saddle, she was the soul of decorum, disregarding things that normally would have given her a start. She was used in a team only when there was a real need.

Papa had acquired an unusually large mule, sleek, strong and opinionated. Papa had a "hand" with horses and many a time he was called to assist in persuading a balky horse to start working again when it had refused to obey its owner. With a very small hammer Papa would tap lightly on the underside of a hoof which he steadied between his knees. Usually that would do the job. Papa never had to "break" any of his colts. They were handled, petted, babied, and made accustomed to halters, surcingles, saddles or baby-sized harness from their earliest days. Jinny, the mule, was something else! On altogether too many nights we would be aroused by a terrific crashing noise at the barn. Like all good irrigators, Papa kept his high-topped rubber boots at the side of his bed and Mama said that when the racket broke loose at the barn, he had his boots on and was going out of the back door pulling his overall straps up over his shoulders as he went, before she could believe that he had even one boot in place! Usually Jinny was out in the corral before Papa could run to the barn. It seemed that Papa was always having to mend the hay manger or the barn door!

One day when there was disc-harrowing to be done, there were only two work horses available—a trusty, calm pair of bays much like English "Shires." Papa gave them the inside position because of their dependability. Dandelion had the left side, which left Jinny for the right, on the theory that the driver's hand on the right would be more firm and persuasive than the one of the left. As it happened, there was no need for a firm hand on the teams, at least not at first...Jinny balked!! Nothing that I could say to her or no slapping of the reins would change her mind, but with every rein-slap Dandelion flinched and tried to lean into the collar with Ned and Maud, the two bays, to move the harrow. When Papa realized that the harrow had not come around the loop of the discing as it should, he came looking for us. There we sat, and no persuasive or authoritative voice could change Jinny's mind. Apparently Papa had no desire to try to tap one of *her* hooves as he had done with the neighbors' horses. At last, Papa, who never hit a horse, had an inspiration. We were stalled by the side of an old headgate, that must have been in place since the first laterals had been put in. He suddenly gave the board a yank. It came out easily. "Get a grip on those reins," said Papa. With that, he raised the headgate and swung it. Right down onto Jinny's satin-smooth hip it went. The rotten old wood promptly broke, making a sharp snap. Ned and Maud seemed to think justice was being done, so they moved forward together calmly and steadily. Dandelion thought it a good idea to try to jump completely out of her harness, but steadied by the middle horses, began to pull. Jinny? The minute she heard the cr-r-ack of that old rotten board, she went to work! We made the trip around the field much faster than usual, but when we neared Papa again and I said "Whoa," four obedient animals came to a halt. As I recall it, that was the only time that Jinny ever balked!!

That same summer another incident was part fun, part "too bad." We had a hired man who was young and good-looking. Also Mama had a hired girl helping her. As part of Hetty's duties, she helped do the washing, which was a bit relieved from its unpleasant nature by the fact that Hetty wanted to impress the hired man with what a worker she was (which was natural!) At that time, there was a new brand of underwear for men. It was known as "Porous Knit" and was supposed to possess a lot of good qualities including being lightweight, *really porous* and cool, and easy to wash. Papa said the hired man was very proud of his new "Porous Knit" when he and the other men peeled off their outer shirts. After the week's supply of clothes had been soaped and washed in the clothes boiler and dumped into one of the large tubs for scrubbing on a clothes board, Mama heard a muffled combination of a scream, a laugh, and weeping. We ran to see what was going on. There stood Hetty beside the washboard. In her hands she held the "Porous Knit" which by this time was *truly* porous. It slid from one hand to the other in a sticky mass and no matter how Hetty tried to pull it together, it still slipped and slid and fell through her fingers onto the surface below. She was almost in hysterics and the hired man was furious when he came up from the field and saw the remains of what had once been a source of pride. Poor Hetty!

CHAPTER 5

Now at this time, Papa and Mama were faced with the same situation that they had seen other parents face during the year in Pendleton when students came to our house and shared Mama's "coaching" and her advice at a time when sons and daughters of farmers had to leave home in order to go to high school. Julian was ready for the 9th grade!

At that time in Weiser, Idaho, there was an excellent boarding school for farm boys and girls. It was "Idaho Industrial Institute," known as "I.I.I." Students worked on the school farm one-half day, and went to

Living at the I.I.I.
Here We See Julian and his Roommate, Studying and Doing the Laundry

classes for one-half day. The president of the school was Dr. Paddock who was another of those rare people—a combination of fine teacher, pastor, and advisor. After Weiser, Julian attended school at Nyssa High School. At this time he acted as night operator for the telephone company which serviced the adjacent farming areas as well as the town. He lost quite a bit of sleep, but the farmers usually went to bed quite early so there were fewer calls coming through the "board" than if he had been on a day shift. He had a cot that he could use "through the small hours" provided he did not miss any incoming calls. The manager and his wife tried to arrange for meals, but we noticed that as a farm boy accustomed to farm meals, he weighed less than he ordinarily would have, had he been home. But he was pleased to have this 'phone job which meant the difference between school and no school.

Julian finished his high school work at Payette, Idaho, which school had been recommended by teachers at I.I.I. During holidays on the farm he and Mama shared a part of his school work in that he began debating, an activity that he continued into his years at O.A.C. (Oregon Agricultural College, later Oregon State College.) I well remember the pleasure they shared when they took turns presenting the "Affirmative" and the "Negative" on topics for debate, with Julian usually doing the rebuttals. It was wonderful training for him as Mama insisted on proper speech, and good use of his voice, as well as knowledge of the subject matter. Debating was a time-consuming but enjoyable activity for him.

Both Mama and Julian looked ahead to his majoring in Agronomy in college (this was the art and science of crop production), which would be of inestimable value to a farmer. They both agreed that when this course was completed he should get some training in law, thus following a family tradition from Mama's family. While these things were going on in Julian's schooling he was away from home during the years when I was getting more acquainted with the Owyhee, Warren (Hogback), and Kingman Kolony neighborhoods. The six years' difference between his age and mine put us into different circles of friendships and activities, but he was always thoughtful of his little "Sis" and I, in turn, was tremendously proud of my big brother.

In the first years on the farm, I learned to be a "listener" as well as a "doer" and "watcher." Papa taught me to listen for the sound of an engine—was it running too fast, too slow, or had it stopped? I learned to listen for the cow bells when Prince and I had been sent to bring the cows back to the farm from uncultivated areas where they had been grazing. I listened to the sound of the big threshing machine coming our way, was it one mile away, two miles away? This gave me information to relay to Papa. An errand done in the evening, taking me to a farm aross the river, with the return expected to be made before dark, taught me a safety signal. I was such a coward about running water, unless I could see the stream bottom! Papa taught me to head Prince or Dandelion as the case might be, to the correct shallow crossing, then to sit quietly while I listened for the riffle of the water where it poured over the rocks so that I could make my crossing wherever I wanted as soon as the horse was satisfied as to the proper footing.

Our farmhouse had three bedrooms and the west window in my room opened toward the large lateral from the "big ditch." It followed our property line and in warm weather on still nights the little frogs in the water and weeds set up choruses of small but exceedingly musical voices. However, one late evening there was a most horrible contrast to the beauty of the frog's songs. There was suddenly the thud of heavy board and the snap off a whip on a horse's hips. Once heard, those sounds always would be recognized. Again and again came the blows. I tried to cover my ears to kill the sound, but it was too late. The blows were coming from one of the farms not far away. There was no escaping them. Quoting from C.S. Lewis again, "One of the most terrible noises in the world...a horse's scream..."

It was amazing to experience cruelty and kindness so close together as they were in our neighborhood. One summer it became apparent that a family living in a shack above the ditch was without proper clothing or food. Discreet questioning showed that they were destitute. A few 'phone calls from one neighbor to another found Mama chosen to get in touch with the county Board of Commissioners to learn whether there might be any funds (a *few* dollars) that could be made available for sheet and pillow case material and for a few towel-lengths that the women of our community could sew into proper sizes. The amount of money available was small, but when it was augmented by donations, even though they, too, were small, it provided a new outlook on life for the family. The men provided a job for the father and supplies of food for all.

Inevitably there were illnesses, deaths and funerals. There were weddings and births. The schoolhouse was the center for the surprisingly many get-togethers, from elections, to Christmas and Easter celebrations. There were "box socials." There were Grange meetings. Above and beyond all else, there were Sunday School and church services, with a few "revivals" thrown in for good measure. The nearby cemetery, or graveyard, was like a record of the families of the community.

On each Memorial Day (or "Decoration Day" as it was called) for several years after we moved to the farm, Grandma Bradley came to our house in her buggy with her trusty horse pulling it. Then, with her granddaughter Maudie Clark and me by her side, she took us first to one or two farms where there were old-fashioned yellow or pink roses and "flags" (purple iris) for the taking; then she would take us and the flowers to the scattered graves that she knew about around the area. Last of all we stopped at the cemetery which in those early days really was a graveyard. There we deposited the last of our flowers. The individual graves were always mounded, and covered with what we called "river rocks" to prevent, or at least to deter, defacement of the graves by animals. It was a grim-looking place, but as time went by, the scattered graves were transferred to it and, by the combined efforts of the people in the community, the present well-cared-for cemetery was brought into being. Research had to be done to learn some of the names and the data for the scattered graves before they could be moved. Mama worked hard on this, as did many of the other women. Considerable writing was involved and much physical labor by the men plus the raising and allocation of funds to insure the proper loving care that has been lavished on this now-handsome memorial ground.

The installation of the Grange in the neighborhood brought some new activities of several types. There was the excitement and the drama of initiation procedures with the use of names and symbolism from Greek mythology. There were the delicious refreshments or suppers for the families of the members. The business meetings dealt with problems of production and of marketing which of course were of intense interest. Papa developed quite an interest in the problems of the orchardists and I followed him as he used his magnifying instruments to find and identify pests. It was a Grange project and was a practical and helpful one. Some of the men specialized in hay-marketing and tried, not always successfully, to persuade the Grangers to hold together for a uniform price per ton. The County Grange was called Pomona Grange. One year Papa was the "Master" and was the delegate to the State Convention in Roseburg, Oregon. Mama and I went with him an I stayed with a distant cousin while the convention was in session. Oregon's young Governor West was the "star" of the speakers' list. For months after this meeting he was in the public eye as an outstanding advocate of the Initiative, Referendum and Recall. It was a good lesson in political science for all three of us from

Malheur County Pomona, and it was a good lesson in geography and in Oregon history for me. Mama saw to it what we were permitted to visit and inspect one of the sleek passenger boats that anchored on the Willamette River in Portland or cruised on the Columbia.

Back at home, election days were days of excitement whether they were general election days or merely school board elections. Voters were brought in from wherever they might be, even from out on the range, and their credentials carefully checked. Mama always saw to it that food was provided for the election workers or anyone else on hand at lunch time.

Religious life in the community was varied. It is surprising that there was much unanimity since there were so many differences of opinion among the 'believers.' Strangely, it may have been those same differences that held them together, because they preferred to have worship services of different kinds than to have none. They tried to look for unity in the sermons and Sunday School lessons rather than to emphasize their differences. True it was, that the 'quarterly' for adult studies was labeled "The Methodist"...but if there needed to be differences of opinion pointed out, there were individuals representing other churches who could "set the record straight."

Among the faithful regulars who provided teachers for the classes, quartets to sing at funerals, or 'directors' who worked with the school teachers to provide holiday celebrations, were the Moreys. Both of them were singers and Mrs. Morey (Ella) was the clerk and treasurer for church and Sunday school as well as for the school board. She it was who ordered the books for the school library and a good job she did, providing books for the different grade levels. Grandpa Pinkston and his wife were nearly always present at meetings. One of their daughters was Mrs. Bill Smith. Bill took his turn at being 'superintendent.' Joe Robertson helped whenever there was a revival. The Bradleys, especially 'Grandma' could always be depended upon to participate in discussions, as did Mama.

The "Preachers" came, in turn. Usually the first and third Sundays belonged to the Methodist minister who came from Nyssa. The Presbyterian came on the second Sunday and the Baptist minister came quite regularly on the fourth Sunday. After a few years Nyssa supplied also a Nazarene preacher who came on the fifth Sunday or any "open" Sunday. About the only time that differences in beliefs were apparent was during a revival. Finally, I became bothered by these differences and questioned

Mama. Her reply was easily understood. She said, "What is it that all of the differences *agree* on?" "They all want to go to Heaven," said I. "All right," said Mama, "If you wanted to go for groceries," (flour, sugar, staples in quantity), "where would you go?" "I'd go to Nyssa." "How would you get there?" "Oh, I'd go by the ditch-bank road, or the straight road from the Owyhee store, or out through the sagebrush road." "There's your answer," said Mama. "For groceries or God, there are choices of ways to do it." I got the idea.

I blithely played the organ for all of the different services without worrying about the denominations. It didn't bother me even when Grandma Bradley told Mama that she and I would probably not make it to heaven because we were Episcopalians, and *they* permitted dancing and some other definite sins, such as playing cards like "500" or "Pinochle!" My most shocking experience at church was in having one of the organ pedal straps break while a song was in progress...once at a funeral! This required "double-time pumping" with one foot, on the remaining pedal. Papa made the repairs "between times."

Silas ("Si") and Gertie Bigelow were stalwarts of the Sunday School and church. Si took many turns as Superintendent and Gertie was always on hand when any work needed to be done or music planned. Before long, their daugher Juanita was doing an inspiring job as organist, or pianist—when a piano was purchased. Silas was quiet and reassuring. At one time in my adult years when I was visiting Si and Gertie, and was troubled over a problem that I thought I couldn't solve, I didn't even have to tell him. Silas sensed that I was troubled. For many years after that I carried in my purse a quotation that he handed to me at that time. "In all thy ways acknowledge Him an He will direct thy paths." Si and Gertie believed in putting their beliefs into practice. One of the Owyhee ministers was a sweet little old man, who was sent to our area. He had no salary, but he had a faith in God. Si and Gertie took him into their home and cared for him. Theirs was the only home he had. He did get into trouble on one matter, however. One Sunday we sang, "I shall know my Redeemer when I reach the other side; And His smile will be the first to welcome me." At the close of the song, the frail, white-haired little lonely-looking man made a comment that referred to his wife and their "togetherness" in years gone by, hoping that when he "reached the other side" she, too, would be there waiting for him. Some said that the remark was not according to true Bible teachings, but I thought (even at that tender age) that it was a from-the-heart expression of appreciation and love, and that God would understand. One summer night the little minister died, there at Silas' and Gertie's home. Si and Papa and another neighbor did the preliminary preparations for burial. I think he reached Heaven with no problem.

At the other end of the age scale, we once had a very young unmarried minister who lived in Nyssa with his widowed mother and a mid-teenage handsome young brother. The brother, in hunting season, climbed through a barbed-wire fence. His gun caught on the wire, discharged, and he was killed. The next Sunday we had no minister, but he came to us the following Sunday. His text was from Matthew: "My Father, if it be possible, let this cup pass from me; nevertheless, not as I will but as Thou wilt."

At one time there was an attempt to stimulate attendance at Sunday School by offering a nice little round pin as a reward for perfect attendance. Different periods of time were indicated by different metals from which the pins were made, until a full year was completed and a gold pin awarded. I was amazed that Mama did not approve the scheme. She had learned long ago to make and sell hair switches which were tremendously popular. She had been taught by a woman who had learned the craft in Germany before coming to the United States. From this work Mama had a *small* income but she was willing to draw upon it for special donations. Thus, she was willing to pay her share for the attendance pins, but she objected to the plan on several grounds. She maintained that the perfect attendance requirement did not offer the right incentive. In her eyes, the plan emphasized health only, whereby practically no one could fulfill the 52 perfect Sundays unless the pupil attended when he or she should have been in bed at home, or at if able to be out of bed, should not have been scattering germs to other pupils.

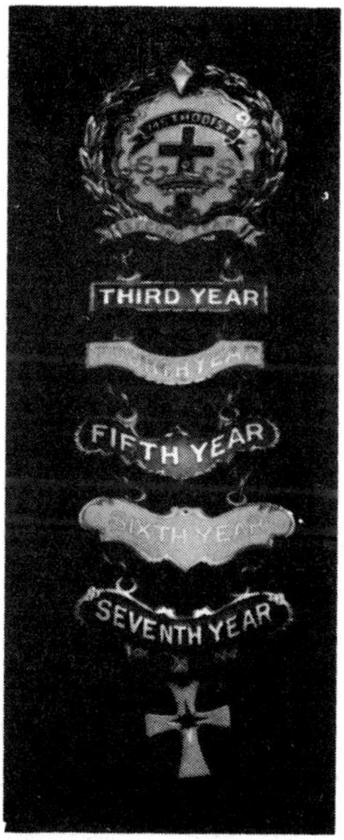

Marian's Sunday School Pin

Also, Mama wanted the pupils to *want* to *attend* Sunday School, not merely to get a pin. Mama proposed a plan which was adopted; a plan that put the responsibility directly on the pupil, namely, that Sunday School would be attended unless it were impossible. Thus, if there were any question as to whether it might be the fault of the pupil that an absence was recorded, it was fairly simple, as well as good training, for the boy or girl to ask him—or herself, "Could I have gone to Sunday School that day?" If a family had to be on a train on Sunday, that would constitute an excused absence. Sickness counted for an excused absence. Arrival of the threshers on a Sunday, counted for an excused day, if the men had to be fed. If one were visiting where there was no Sunday School (yes, it happened in some places), that was excused. Anyway the pupil concerned had to do some honest calculation, or "soul searching" as we called it. It would be interesting to know how many of the little pins were awarded. I recall arriving from Portland from Corvallis one Sunday morning, traveling by train. I think I was eleven years old. I went to the lady in charge of Travelers' Aid in the depot, and asked to be directed to the nearest church which proved to be about one-half to three-fourths of a mile away, along a straight street. At the church I presented a little notebook that I carried, and asked the Sunday School superintendent to sign a statement saying that I had been present in Sunday School that day. So, I had no absence listed against me—not even an excused one. It was a good experience for me from several points of view, *and* Mama was proud of me!

As to school work—by the time I was in the eighth grade I was the only pupil in that grade and my "classes" didn't get called up for recitations during the winter months. In March, a Miss Isabella Eskridge became the teacher and again I had superior teaching. Like our county school superintendent, Fay Clark Hurley, Miss Eskridge spent much time at our house. Between March and the closing of the school in May, she covered with me all of the school work required of an eighth grader in the entire year, and both she and I felt that I was prepared for the state examinations that all eighth graders had to pass...and I did pass them. I became introduced to *Current Events*, which was the mini-sized newspaper for upper-grade pupils. Mama and Papa took the *Review of Reviews* (Adult-sized current-events), the *Kansas City Star* newspaper, plus the *Denver Post*, the *Portland Oregonion*, the *Delineator, Cosmopolitan* and several other papers and magazines. Julian, in his high school manual training class, had built a good-looking, sturdy, large table for our books and papers to lie upon for instant use. There, too, was the Bible for general reading and for reference for the Sunday School lessons.

Rumor had it that more land, especially that in the "bowl" near Mitchell Butte would soon be opened for homesteading. The plan to put a dam across the river at the butte which would serve as the main dam for a reservoir in the bowl had been abandoned because there was not sufficient rock base to hold back the impounded water. So, on the Lowe's reading table there was a copy of *Lord's Oregon Laws* and in the house there frequently were people, both neighbors and strangers, who came to read, study and have Mama explain the regulations or ask Papa to "stake out" their claims. The big unabridged dictionary on an easel had been available for reference work for several years. It was more than available—it was required work for the family and anyone else who wanted to settle an argument on meaning or pronunciation. Mama always explained so far as we children were concerned, that she had not the time to *tell* us about those things and the dictionary could do it better and faster than she, so "Look it up in the dictionary" was a familiar remark.

Tom and Flora Lowe
50th Anniversary
1940

CHAPTER 6

Mama and Papa suddenly realized that they had a twelve-year-old in their family, this time their daughter, who was ready for high school—which again meant leaving home. In modern verbiage, Papa might have said, "Over my dead body!" and Mama felt the same. For two full years I remained at home with high school somewhere in the future, but those two years were packed with all kinds of activities. There was no time to be bored. First of all, because of the lax regulations about who could go to school—or not go—with the teacher's consent, I was allowed to "review" my eighth grade work. This made for a year-long period of enrichment and no time was wasted. O.A.C.'s Extension Department's representatives came with 4-H club work! Mr. Seymour, Mr. Maris and Miss Helen Cowgill were the fore-runners, traveling constantly around the state to explain to parents and students the possibilities and the value of the many projects that were available. Mama was the organizer in our neighborhood. We worked on individual projects, from calf or pig raising, for example, to canning, preserving, pickling and sewing, keeping careful records of all procedures and expenses, plus income and evaluations.

Our county agent, Mr. Howard, was an overseer for the boys and Fay Clark Hurley urged us to sign up for projects. Miss Cowgill made several visits to the Owyhee in the summer, staying at our home, and Mama encouraged all of us to more and more effort. Charley Newbill was chosen by our combined groups to be the president and presided at all meetings. Mama saw an opportunity to help us learn some very simple applications of correct by-law procecures. We were proud of our officers and the way they conducted the meetings. I took the canning project and many of the women of the area helped me by having me can their products in their homes to give me experience with many different foods for use in the coming winter. Each woman graded my work as to its quality (did it "keep?") and its appearance. I canned two hundred eighty-seven jars of fruit, vegetables and meats to meet 4-H requirements, processing a total of five hundred nineteen quarts that summer. I've always thought that, when I received a state award, those lovely women should have had special awards, too for their encouragement and patience with me. Helen Peck, who sewed beautifully, won county and state awards more than once. If we completed our projects we exhibited at county and state fairs, which was always fascinating.

Four-H was predominantly summertime work. Winters in my two years of no-high-school also held a great deal of interest. The Oregon State Library, under devoted and highly trained librarians, was getting books to outlying "stations" all around the state and we were fortunate enough in the Owyhee District to be regular recipients of some of those shipments. According to Cornelia Marvin Pierce who was the first secretary of the Oregon State Library commission, books at first were sent by express to all who asked for them, until the parcel post was started. Ours were sent to Mama and Papa and people came to our house from all around the neighborhood, chose the books they wanted, signed for them and later returned them according to instructions from the headquarters.

It was like having Christmas when the boxes of books arrived. We hurried through with the chores on those days so that we could begin reading. In one of those two no-school winters Papa read aloud to us instead of "fiddling" and it was hard to decide which type of evening we enjoyed the most. One winter we received pictures, which Papa and Mama carried around to all three of our nearby schoolhouses. Papa was in charge of the projector, Mama provided a smooth, taut sheet on which to show the pictures and frequently I provided the script, giving a running account of what we were seeing. Apparently we all enjoyed those late afternoon or evening sessions, but they demanded considerable time and effort on the part of Papa and Mama. Harnessing the horses, driving to our destination, doing our "show," driving home again, took a lot of energy from hard-working farmers. There was a limited choice of pictures available. In addition to that I preferred looking at the truly beautiful pictures that I could see at home, gazing at them through the three-dimensional stereoscope that was one of the "regulars" on the big table, so we discontinued the "Pictures-on-a-Sheet" as we sometimes called them.

Two projects of mine that were related to the two-year period after I completed my eighth grade work, were related both to the Sunday School and to individuals. The first was work on developing a "Cradle Roll." There were several children of various ages in the area, especially quite young ones. These I visited on horseback or on foot, enrolling them in my special booklet and leaving each with a card bearing the name, birth date, and enrollment date. In later years the youngest member of the Bill Smith family (Leonard Smith) who had been duly enrolled as one of my flock, became the first renter on the Hot Springs farm after it became mine. I think this Cradle Roll experience made a special tie and a link of understanding between us.

The second project, which was interesting for me, was my excursion into the field of teaching music. Annie Schweizer was my pupil. Her mother, Mrs. Gus Schweizer, had much more confidence in me than I had in myself, but both Annie and I had a good time. I remember that she had an unusual dog (a house-type in a farm background) so *it* probably received as much attention as did the music! She took me to see the early stages of work that had been done on the house that her father had begun to build, and on which he labored for so long. No one could deny that he was aware of many improvements in living arrangements that could be included in homes. I hope that he lived to see them become commonplace.

With so many things to do, it was no wonder that the two no-school years were soon almost over, and we were faced again with the high school problem. Papa said that even if he could afford it, he wouldn't pay room and board for any 13- or 14-year-old girl in a town at least ten miles away from home! So, I went to Nyssa to live with Paul and Helen Brainard of Payette, Idaho and their baby boy, when Paul was principal of the high school in Nyssa and probably also superintendent of schools. Both Paul and Helen were fine musicians. Paul had a beautiful tenor voice. He had advanced vocal training in New York and a few years later was the tenor soloist with the choir in the Stanford University Memorial Church. Helen was an expert pianist and later was the pipe-organist at a church in Pasadena. Both the Brainards had also had training at the Conservatory at Whitman College in Walla Walla, Washington. It was an excellent place for a young girl to live and "work for her board." In addition to his music, Paul had real skill in the teaching of Ancient History and Elementary Psychology in the high school.

The teacher of Latin and English in Nyssa High School was Althea Sheldon who was also a trained librarian. She taught an interested class of girls to care for the books in the school library and to write "library hand." Her family lived in the Kingman Kolony in the red house originally used as a school when Delva St. Clair did her first teaching, which was in that district. Delva later taught at Creston and she gave up her Squatter's-Rights land near Mitchell Butte in trade for land in the Creston area where she met John Wall. Later they were married at our house on the farm, with Florence Kingman and I as attendants, and they had four boys who were like grandchildren to my parents.

After my year of high school at Nyssa with the Brainards, Papa and Mama realized there were three of us girls in the Owyhee area who wanted to go to high school. We knew each other very well and lived quite close together. There were Martha Moses who became a nurse and now lives in Portland, Oregon, and Gladys Kygar whose family's home was just across the "big ditch" from the Morey's and not much farther than that from our farm. In Nyssa there was a nice little apartment house across the street from the Presbyterian Church. Miss Sheldon and Alice McFarland, the "math" teacher at the high school, each lived in an apartment in the building, with an empty apartment between them. The arrangement was perfect for us to rent the empty one so we had "chaperones"—if any were needed! Our parents provided much food from the farms. All in all, it was the least expensive and best arrangement imaginable. Papa and Mama weren't too happy, however, when I announced that at the high school "No one says 'Papa' and 'Mama'." Everyone said 'Dad' and 'Mother,' or perhaps 'Mom.' But they were understanding parents, so 'Dad' and 'Mother' were accepted.

At the end of my second year at Nyssa High School when the Brainards had returned to their home in Payette, Paul Brainard became interested in Kansas State University in Manhattan, Kansas, and from that time (summer 1918) for about a year, I stayed with them to help Helen take care of their two children while Paul inspected the college with a view to taking a position on the faculty in the psychology department. In the fall, I was to attend Payette High as Julian had done. When my credits from Nyssa were inspected, it was found that I had enough credits to enter Payette High School as a senior. I had taken a number of extra courses at Nyssa and by taking one extra course in Payette I would be able to graduate in the spring of 1919, after only three years of high school. So I "made up" one of those two years following the no-school period after the 8th grade.

At the time Delva was trading land parcels, she and my parents realized that Julian was old enough to file on a claim on a piece of suitable land. Mother filed a "desert claim" on the parcel that Delva traded, and Julian filed a homestead claim on the land nearest the butte on its low side, where the hot spring surfaced. He and Dad and some additional helpers moved Delva's squatter' claim house to a new location on what was now

Julian's homestead near the spring. They split the house into two sections, placed them side by side, added a porch, some trees, and began a continuing series of improvements. The most noticeable and perhaps the most valuable, was that Julian scooped out an area back of the house and built a bank around it to retain water from the spring that was piped to this little reservoir or pond, and of course to the house. There was enough "fall" to the area so that the different levels around the house could be terraced and the water ditched to these levels so that vegetables and flowers and shrubs and more trees could grow...and, a lawn!

Instead of going to college as soon as he finished high school, Julian did this "stint" of homesteading, then went to "O.A.C." During the summer there was plenty of work to do on his homestead, but being young and strong there was always time for a little bit of fun. Nearly everyone who came to visit wanted to climb Mitchell Butte (El. 3502') which was

"The Monument" at the Top of Mitchell Butte. Instruments to Measure Rain, etc. Were Placed Here by the Federal Government

high enough to be challenging, but low enough so that it was a "possible" climb. From the farthest upper peak there was a fascinating view of the entire Owyhee area and on to the mountains beyond Boise where "Squaw Butte" resembled the huge body of a woman lying full length with her

Julian and the Homestead at Mitchell Butte

arms crossed over her breast. On winter evenings the setting sun bathed the snow-covered Squaw Butte in rose colored light that made a beautiful sight. In summer Squaw Butte was a handsome distant landmark from our butte, and those who climbed Mitchell Butte felt well rewarded for their

The Point of Mitchell Butte at the Hot Springs

effort even when there was no snow. A small rock monument capped Mitchell Butte and assured a 360° view. Among those who came to visit Mitchell Butte and Julian were Corrinne Maxwell, Martha Overstreet,

"Climbing the Butte"
From Left to Right: The Grade School Teacher, Helen Peck, Corinne Maxwell, Bob Overstreet, Julian Lowe
Martha Overstreet in Foreground
1916

H.R. Scott, Helen Peck, Bob Overstreet and usually whatever young woman might have been the Kolony teacher.

At about this time Dad and Mother began a series of changes in the management of our farm, renting it to several different couples, including at one time the Walls (Delva St. Clair and her husband John Wall) and their children. To insure the proper care of Julian's homestead (the hot springs-Mitchell Butte land), Dad and Mother moved to Julian's house. The only items that I remember distinctly in the move were gunny sacks or grain sacks stuffed with books and magazines! Dad wasn't too happy when he found what was in the sacks, but Mother, Delva and I would have been heartbroken without them, so Dad ceased his protest and brought more and more. Besides, the big table that Julian had made was in position again as it had been before, so of course it needed books on top of it!

Julian was at O.A.C. in part of 1916-17 and again in the year of 1917-18. Like college campuses all over the United States, O.A.C. was alive with talk of war...the imminence of World War I. It was a chilling

Julian and his Friend Sam Driver (Later Federal Judge Driver) at Camp Louis

Training For War

1918

thought. Dad and Mother knew, from their parents, of the horrors of the Civil War. Some of their ancestors' histories dated back to the Revolution and various "small wars" in between. And now, war again touched their family! Hundreds of Oregon and Washington young men, among them, Julian, left college and were sent to Camp Lewis, Washington, for training; probably for overseas duty.

Throughout the entire summer of 1918 there were rallies, each usually with patriotic addresses, pleas for bond sales and much stirring patriotic music. People came from the farms, gathered in available parks or other open spaces, wherever benches and folding chairs could be placed, to listen to more *and more* talk of war, of our duty to do without materials that could be used in the war effort in this country, or sent to Army Headquarters for shipment to Europe. It was only a matter of weeks until Julian was overseas and I was in Payette in high school where the fervor of war was at fever pitch. Julian's letters bore unfamiliar postmarks, nearly all from France.

At Thanksgiving time there was a school holiday long enough for me to make a trip back to Mitchell Butte, to Julian's homestead, and to Dad and Mother. On Thanksgiving weekend, Charley Bradley, Si Bigelow and one or two other friends arrived one evening, saying that they had very bad news. They broke the news as gently as they could, but nothing could soften the cruel fact. Julian had been killed.

I shall never forget Mother's scream. Again the inherent kindness of friends and neighbors from all of the nearby districts, and from many far away areas, where Julian had been known even slightly, were evidenced by visits, offers of help, or by anything they could think of that would show their sympathy and/or be of practical help. In our immediate Mitchell Butte area were the Mendiolas (a wonderful Spanish and Basque family), Fred Klingback, the Huffmans, the Rusts (two unrelated families), the McLaffertys, two Smith families (not related to each other)—more than I can remember by name but can recall by their kindnesses.

And then, I had to return to school in Payette, and Dad and Mother were left to face what was a very difficult period, with neither of their children with them. Delva Wall was invaluable and Bertha Rachenberger spent many a day offering consolation and help. Her little car made its way up and back down along the ditch-bank road regardless of weather, mud or ruts.

There were painfully practical matters to be settled, as is always true following a death in a family. These were particularly poignant when they related to those men of the Ninety First Wild West Division in France who attacked and took the town of Gesnes (14 miles northwest of Verdun and 150 miles east of Paris), in which struggle, because of the terrible slaughter, it was almost impossible to find eye witness details of deaths. It has been said that if a report said simply that the soldier lost his life in "going to Gesnes" no further explanation need be made. Due to the efforts of the searchers connected with the Red Cross, and to friends who were in that charge, it was finally found in which part of the Gesnes attack Julian was wounded and the field hospital where he received first treatments and then died. It was possible for his family to be contacted and given the choice of where his last resting place would be. Dad and Mother decided that his body would be returned to the United States and after heart-rending study, Arlington National Cemetery was chosen as the appropriate

The First Markers at Arlington National Cemetery in 1922
These were Replaced in the 1930's by Permanent Stone Markers

place for interment, there among hundreds and hundreds of his "buddies"—honored dead. Later on, a much appreciated memorial was made to Julian in our own Malheur County, at Vale, Oregon, on the grounds of the courthouse. The first Legion Post in the county was organized in Vale and was named for him as the county's first casualty in World War I.

The next decision-making that was necessary had to do with the legalities of Julian's homestead. There were a few items that remained to be settled, as is always the case in finishing a "claim." These had to do with the death of the original "filer" (Julian.) Who was now responsible? Dad and Mother were notified that if they (the "nearest of kin") would complete the technicalities, practical and legal, that might have remained had Julian returned, title to the land would be granted to them. Both from the sentimental point of view that this would have been Julian's, and from their own love of the area and of this "claim" in particular, they immediately set out to, and did, complete all requirements. Within a few months after they were granted title, they deeded the place to me, with a "life time lease" back to them.

In their remaining years their chief object was to continue to improve the land and to make an enjoyable home on the Mitchell Butte Hot Springs land. On their original Owyhee farm they had been so busy that crops, of course, took precedence over flowers, but at this Hot Springs home the little reservoir, or pond, that Julian had constructed had ample water for the area around the house for grass, vegetable garden, terraces on the north and south for vines and flowers. Mother seeded hollyhocks that made a riot of color and some unusual plants found Mother's care and the soil to their liking. A number of these came from a nursery in Toppenish, Washington, which was owned and operated by Bert Sturm, one of the Pendleton group of boys who had spent time with "the Lowes" so many years before and who always called Mother "Ma."

In approximately six years after Julian's death when I had completed college and a year of high school teaching and had married, my husband (Carl Quackenbush) and I visited the Oregon farm and from that visit there sprang an enduring affection and admiration between those two—my mother and my husband. Carl was a high school football coach and history teacher and, in addition, was already eager to study law in his 'spare' time. His background was that of a Minnesota farm boy. His mother was born in Norway, her family one of those hardy and adventuresome groups who came to the United States in search of a new way of life. The Quackenbush side of Carl's background was Holland Dutch, stemming from the Dutch groups who had settled in New York in the first waves of those who had come for land, and for independence. Carl's father used to say, "The Quackenbushes 'married Dutch' all the way down the line, until I married my little Norwegian girl!"

Mother was especially interested in Carl's determination to attend Law School. At first he took courses in summer school at Stanford and the University of California, but soon took full-time night classes in Spokane which meant that he was one of the group of adult students in Law School who were earning their way with daytime teaching jobs (many of them coaches), or by other work, by refereeing football games all around the area and in the summer being a life guard at one or another of the swimming pools operated by Spokane's Park Board.

Mother's additional interest was, of course, in our children, Marian, Derce, and Justin. Every summer we managed to get down to the farm and sometimes it "took a bit of doing." We always said that we helped to build the highway all of the way—mile by mile—frequently behind a Highway Department "lead-car." All of us believed that the visit was worth the effort. I know that Mother and Dad had new interests in life because of those visits. One summer all three children stayed for three weeks without us. Delva Wall came and brought her youngest son who was a joy to all. Another summer Justin ("Bud" as we called him at that time) stayed alone

Model T Ford
Note Canvas Water Bag on the Door. This was a Typical Sight for those Working Their Way Across the Desert
Summer of 1925

with his grandparents and his letters indicated how much he learned. Dad even provided a pony for him!

By 1932 Carl had completed Law School, had passed the State Bar Examinations and had been appointed a Deputy Prosecuting Attorney for Spokane County. By 1940 he was appointed Prosecuting Attorney, which position he held until he went into the Army, in World War II, commissioned-in as a Major in Military Government. When the war was over he returned as Prosecuting Attorney and in 1946 he became a Judge of the Superior court of Spokane County, Washington, retiring in 1958 after 12 years on the bench.

Mother was always one of Carl's most ardent admirers and supporters. From her interest in his career and the education and careers of the various young people she had known, including her children and grandchildren, came her general interest in education, especially as evidenced in the work of the Parent Teacher Association. She often mentioned her pleasure in these young people, especially Delva St. Clair

Wall, Gordon MacLafferty, Herman Rust, Juanita Bigelow Jungquist, Mildred Hite Elliot, Ethel Morey Logan and many others.

In April, 1939, the Ontario paper carried a report of a talk given by Dr. F.A. Macomber of the University of Oregon on "Progressive Education" at the Malheur County Parent-Teachers meeting. We quote: "The soundness of these so-called progressive ideas of modern pedagogy were forcefully and delightfully presented to the meeting of the Malheur County Parent-Teachers last Saturday by Dr. Macomber of the University of Oregon; but it was no surprise to some of the older persons present to hear Mrs. Tom Lowe of the Owyhee community explain that the program he was urging, was to a degree, that which was followed by the progressive teachers in the old country schools of many years ago. It was inspiring, too, to hear Dr. Macomber admit that the educator today is realizing that in many of the educational methods of the past there was much which is applicable to teaching today. In other words the educators are examining results secured along the road they have been traveling. Finding them not all they seek, many educators are willing to backtrack in an effort to locate the landmarks to set them again on the trail for the best possible education of the individual, compatible with changed conditions. It is encouraging when there are educators ready to admit that the past was not devoid of its merits...that a return to the old trails might prove beneficial."

As time went by, Mother began receiving requests that she write something on the founding of the Parent-Teacher Association so that the early efforts and the difficulties that were encountered would not be forgotten. The one that was founded was the first in Malheur County. Following is an informal report by Mother about the work that was done to complete the struggles for the Association:

"What drove me to do something was that the men school board members were so satisfied with themselves because they saved money for the district by hiring the cheapest teachers to be found...those who either had never taught or had been so ineffectual where they taught that they couldn't get the same school again, so they would teach for very little pay. Well, I had always been interested in the Mother's Congress from its beginning. I had tried to get Pendleton women to organize a Mother's Congress Circle, but even Mrs. Coleworthy knew practically nothing of it and they were engrossed in the work of the Tuesday Afternoon Club. Time went on and we came to this county chasing the promised "High Line

Ditch" under the hoped-for Owyhee dam, and the school chosen by chance was a surprise. I had never dreamed a rural school would be so far from helpful. The talks and the explanations I inflicted on this long-suffering district finally bore fruit however. I had written to Portland and received a national year book of Mothers' Congress, giving names of national officers to whom I wrote. They sent such a pitifully inadequate bunch of pamphlets, but still I gathered something. Then I wrote again to the Portland Corresponding Secretary who wrote to me that a Mrs. Landers, wife of the City Superintendent of Pendleton Schools might be able to give me information. But, of course, before that I had written to the County Superintendent of Malheur County telling him there were so many children who stayed home from school, some with their parents' knowledge and some who started to school but instead played and visited each other. I asked him if he didn't believe a Mothers' Congress that could get together with the teachers and talk over the truant proposition would be helpful. They could help each other to stand for better attendance and better teachers. He wrote that he knew nothing of the Mothers' congress nor why it had begun, but as to trying to compel people to keep their children in school every day of the school term, his advice was that there was always trouble enough in rural schools without trying to make parents raise their children according to other people's ideas...and his idea was for anyone to 'let sleeping dogs lie.'

"Then I wrote to the County Superintendent of Union County at La Grande, as well as several other county superintendents asking what were the requirements to become a Standard Rural School. I thought if I could get some of the patrons interested in a better school house and fixtures I might lead on to better teachers. But none of the superintendents knew what the constitution of the Mothers' Congress stood for. Some had heard of Standard Rural School requirements, but didn't know what they were. Meanwhile, a pamphlet now and then would come from Mrs. Landers. Finally, she had found a card of requirements for a standard rural school, from an eastern state. She said it would give me an idea and as soon as Oregon prepared something of the kind she would see that I had instructions. Her husband was city superintendent of Pendleton. I found several in this district so interested in what might be required to be standard, but they feared to start a Mothers' Congress until they knew what members were supposed to do and were afraid the county superintendent might not want a Mothers' Congress organized.

"Finally in 1912 or 1913, five women, Mrs. Morey, Mrs. Bigelow, Mrs. Morg Logan, Mrs. Newbill and Mrs. Eddie Wilson came to our house and we organized a Mothers' Congress. I have forgotten if the locals were called circles or meetings. I was elected President. We met each two weeks. We gave entertainments to pay dues and fill the local treasury. We easily annexed several names when they learned their dues—10¢—were paid out of the treasury. Portland was organized and was state headquarters and had not much literature but sent me what they could. In about a year and a half (I do not remember just how long, but I think it was 1914), I was so surprised to receive notice from the state secretary that I had been elected vice president for the state! I was given three counties as my district.

"After a few years the organization was called 'Oregon congress of Mothers and Parent-Teachers Association.' Then (again, I have forgotten the year), it was named Parent-Teacher organization and the locals are now called Associations instead of Circles as formerly. My life membership was given me by the County Council. I also received a Life Membership paid by the Ontario Auxilliary of American Legion. There were no two-room rural schools, nor was there even one 'Standard' rural school in this county when we organized the Mothers' Congress, but we soon had several standard one-room schools, then standard two-room schools, and teachers who were better prepared."

Mother, Dad and Burt Sturm (Who Owned the Nursery in Toppenish.)

1940

I have always been glad Mother lived to see the Parent-Teachers Organization functioning in Malheur County. There were some events concerning her children and grandchildren that would have pleased her also. Under Patton's Third Army in France, my husband was awarded the bronze Cross of Lorraine and a citation from the citizens of Nancy. The citation, signed by the mayor, stated in part:

> *I desire, in the name of the municipal delegation and of the whole population of the City of Nancy, to express to you our heart-felt thanks. You arrived on the very day of our liberation. You immediately set to work to reorganize the life of the city in an atmostphere of mutual esteem, mixed with gratitude on our part.*
>
> *A great friendship resulted and it is with deep regret that we see you go. Our good wishes accompany you.*
>
> *I give you this cross of Lorraine in token of our friendship:*
>
> Le Maire (The Mayor)

Mother would be delighted that so many of her descendents are working in fields that were of major interest to her and to her ancestors before her. For instance, our older daughter, my namesake, attended Whitman College and graduated from Washington State College (now University.) After her marriage she lived in Wenatchee for about 15 years, where she was the librarian for the school district. She had three daughters—two of them are teachers. Our second daughter, Derce is a teacher in Phoenix. She has four daughters, one of them studying for an advanced degree in psychology. One of them lives in Australia where she and her husband and two children live on, and operate, a small farm; marketing, among a number of other things, carnations! She and her husband met while they were teaching in the University in Brisbane, Queensland. Derce's two younger daughters lead busy lives in business and in caring for their families. These four girls in one winter were scattered all the way from Puerto Rico and Orlando, Florida to Flagstaff, Arizona, Minneapolis, Minnesota, Fort Worth, Texas and Missouri to Australia!

Our third child, Justin, who is our only son, graduated from the University of Idaho, then was on a destroyer during the Korean conflict. After returning to Spokane, which is still his home, he, like his father, studied law in night school. One year ago this summer (1980) he was sworn in as U.S. District (Federal) Court Judge for Eastern Washington. To quote the local newspaper, "...the oath of office being administered by his father, retired Spokane County Superior Court Judge Carl C. Quackenbush." Justin's wife, Polly, who returned to college at 47 to obtain an interdisciplinary masters degree in guidance and counseling and organizational management at Eastern Washington University, teaches classes for returning women students at the University and works in the Women's Programs for Washington Community College District 17 in Spokane. Justin and Polly have three children: Karl, who is a Seattle attorney, did his law school work at the University of Washington. Kathy, one of the youngest of our eight much-loved grand-daughters, attends Spokane Falls Community College. Robert, our youngest grandchild, attends Seattle Pacific University in Seattle, where he is a sophomore.

In looking back over the lives of my parents and of my own family, I realize how joy and sorrow touched all of us. From the days of Grandma Bradley and the flowers in the Owyhee Cemetery, we young ones observed and suffered with many of the adults in the community as they recalled members of their families who were no longer living, especially those who had recently died. The compassion that was developed in us stayed with us and deepened as time went by and we experienced grief and losses in our own lives.

In the spring of 1981 our beloved older daughter, Marian, died after a two-year struggle with cancer. A loving friend has quoted to us from Anne Morrow Lindberg's poem "Pilgrim:"

This is a road one walks alone;
Narrow the track and overgrown.

Dark is the way, and hard to find,
When the last village drops behind.

Never a footfall, light to show
Fellow traveler...yet, I know

Someone before has trudged his load,
In the same footsteps...This is a road.

Another friend helped to give us courage by quoting a prayer that carries the same thought and I, in turn, quote part from it:

"God of our life, there are days...when the road seems dreary and endless...and our hearts are lonely. Flood the path with light...tune our hearts to brave music. So quicken our spirits that we may be able to encourage all who journey with us on the road of life. Amen."

In late October, 1981, after having been in ill health for a number of years, Carl died. One of our U.S. Senators wrote: "All of us in the Pacific Northwest have been enormously proud of [Carl's] tremendous achievements—as a lawyer, judge, teacher, athletic director and outstanding citizen. He contributed much to our state and to our nation."

Long before this, Dad and Mother had died, Mother in 1943 and Dad in 1952. After Mother died, Dad remarried, and had several years of a happy marriage to a kindly, considerate, and handsome widow who made me feel more than welcome to visit them, even showing me that she had kept Mother's silver hand-mirror, brush and comb in their usual position on a chest of drawers so that I would know of her affection for Mother and of her desire to carry forward memories of her.

When Mother died, each of the Malheur county newspapers carried accounts of her life and work in helping to develop the schools of the county and any and all phases of work for the betterment of children of the Owyhee district. One of the papers, I believe the *Gate City Journal* of Nyssa, emphasized a baptism that had been held in the Hot Spring at Mitchell Butte. Another paper wrote especially of her work in P.T.A. and Malheur County Health Association. A third gave attention to her interest in the Kingman Kolony Klub, a reading group with 12 members (for the 12 months of the year), and to the Rev. Mr. Luscombe's summation of her Christian life.

However, the article on page one of the *Malheur Enterprise* of Vale touched all who read it:

"How fitting it was that the last rites for Mrs. Thomas Lowe, Malheur pioneer mother, should have been held in a school house. No cathedral, some present remarked, could have been more appropriate or could have thrown more lustre on the useful life just closed.

"For Mrs. Lowe's first thought was always for the children of Malheur county. All of life interested her—as it does any well-rounded person—but it was the welfare of the children that inspired her greatest enthusiasm. First in her own home—where all good work should start—then in her beloved community of Owyhee; then through the Parent-Teachers' Organization of county and state, Mrs. Lowe fought for those things which would make a better community and a better world for her own and other people's children. She was the 'mother' of the Parent-Teachers' work in Malheur County. She was one of the most active backers for many years of the Owyhee Sunday School. She was one of the little band of eager pioneers who started the Malheur County Public Health Association. She never failed a worthy cause in need of a staunch, informed advocate.

"Her interest in the welfare of the next generation had more to it than merely an ameliorative approach. She looked deeper, seeking the causes of the maladjustment and inequalities in our social order. And this study gave her, as it must any thinking person, a conviction that human values must transcend property values before any lasting improvement can be effected in our ailing society. To some people, this is a radical point of view. To Mrs. Lowe, it was merely logical because, as she saw it, it was Christian.

"The people of Malheur County should pause this week in salute to the memory of a noble and gracious lady. Her like will not pass this way again soon."

INDEX

H

I

J

K

L

M

S

T

U

V

W

Y

COLOPHON

The Marian Lowe Quackenbush AIR, SUNLIGHT AND A BIT OF LAND, *was printed in the workshop of Glen Adams, which is located in the sleepy country village of Fairfield, Washington, southern Spokane County, Washington state. The text pages were set in type by Dale La Tendresse using a Compugraphic 7300 computer photosetter. The text is set in twelve point Baskerville roman with two points of air between the lines. Running heads are in ten point Baskerville Bold italic. Page numbers are twelve point Baskerville Bold. Some minor correctional line setting was done by Miss Kristy Frisbie. General book design and any letterpress imprinting in color is by Glen Adams. Title page lettering is in Baskerville Bold. Camera-darkroom work is by Evelyn Foote Clausen, who, with Miss Kristy Frisbie folded the sheets and assembled the signatures, using a Pitney-Bowes multisheet collator and folder. The sheets were printed by Robert La Tendresse using a 770CD Hamada offset press. Mr. La Tendresse also stripped the film, did necessary opaque work, and made the plates. The paper stock is sixty pound Simpson Opaque in a wove finish. Binding is by Willem Bosch of Oakesdale, Washington. This was a fun project. We had no special difficulty with the work.*